LACE for DOLLS

&

DOLLS' HOUSES

LACE for DOLLS
&
DOLLS' HOUSES

ANN COLLIER

B T Batsford, London

First published in 1997 by

B T Batsford Ltd

583 Fulham Road

London SW6 5BY

A catalogue record for this book is available from the British Library

ISBN 0 7134 8057 2

Printed in Hong Kong

Page 2: Victorian costume with crinoline
Title page: Twelve scale shop

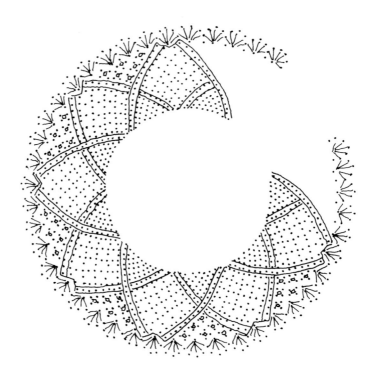

CONTENTS

INTRODUCTION

'The common size of the natives is somewhat under six inches, so there is an exact proportion in all other animals, as well as plants and trees...I have been much pleased with observing a cook pulling a lark, which was not so large as a common fly; and a young girl threading an invisible needle with invisible silk'

Gulliver's Travels, Jonathan Swift

Many children play with dolls, copying their mother in looking after them or organizing them into families and creating stories. They love to dress and undress them over and over again, and they eagerly collect the assorted paraphernalia for their dolls, including a large wardrobe of dresses. This love of dolls dates back hundreds of years – antique dolls are in existence that have been played with by generations of children.

In the adult world, these antique dolls are popular among collectors, and large prices are paid for them, however dilapidated they have become, and great satisfaction is gained by restoring them to their former glory. Indeed, many doll owners treat their dolls like children, providing them with different costumes for different seasons and sometimes even putting them to bed at night in their own night attire. There are also those who make and collect dolls dressed in fashion from different historical periods, and doll-making kits (and ready-made dolls) are available in sizes ranging from 15 cms (6 in) to 61 cms (24 in). The process of creating the costumes, searching for the correct fabric, researching the underclothes and making the patterns is all part of the enjoyment.

In producing this series of doll and dolls' house lace projects, I want to share with you the research that I have done into the various historical periods, the types and colours of the fabrics, the types of lace that were worn, the hairstyles that were fashionable and the reasons why fashion changed. The periods chosen reflect the fact that very little lace was worn before the Elizabethan period. From then on it was used lavishly for some 250 years until it became less fashionable after the First World War.

Elizabethan dress with blackwork sleeves and collar
(see Figs. 1, 2 and 3 and instructions on page 12-13)

Fashion has always been a way of presenting the body by disguising or emphasizing natural contours. The 'bum roll' or the bustle are classic examples of the latter, while tight corsets were once used to narrow the waist. In the past, and in high society, clothes were certainly not influenced by what was practical, unlike many of the clothes worn today. In the earlier periods covered, and among the upper classes, women were decorative objects, their first aim being to attract a man and then as their husband's ornamental possession. In an age with few books and magazines, fashion ideas were transmitted by pictures, fashion dolls or word of mouth. Our knowledge of what these people wore is gained from statues and portraits – but one must always remember that for such a record for posterity, the subjects would have been dressed in their most lavish attire.

In contrast, garments for the working population were much more functional. The poorest people wore filthy, ragged versions of the clothes worn by the prosperous. The clothes were first handed on to serving maids, and then sold on until they finally ended up in the flea markets. As this would take several years, changes in fashion were not obvious or immediate. The middle classes tried to keep up with the trends but in a simplified form.

One can find out what materials were used from the costumes that have survived and from records of bills of purchase.

Fashions often changed to suit house furnishings and sometimes furniture design had to adapt to fashion. At first, most costume was dictated by climatic conditions; gauzy linens in Greece and Rome and fur in the colder climes, but by the sixteenth century fashion was influenced by the French court. And as people began to travel they discovered new materials, such as silks and brocades from the Far East and fine light muslins from India.

Lace was used extensively from the Elizabethan era, but because of its expense it was only worn by the wealthy. Needlelace proved the most popular, although bobbin versions of a similar design were produced and would probably have been cheaper. All lace was regarded as a sign of wealth, just like jewellery, and, in the sixteenth and seventeenth centuries, it was sometimes made with threads of gold and silver. Designs followed the fashion trends and the handmade variety flourished until lacemaking machines were invented in the 1830s. Machine-produced lace made it accessible to the masses and consequently it was never so widely worn or used in house furnishings than during Victorian times.

CHAPTER ONE
40-46 CM (16-18 IN) DOLLS

The Elizabethans

The dress of this period was ornate and as fabric printing was not known, any decoration was embroidered, often in an all-over scroll design with a profusion of realistic plant and animal forms. Black was highly favoured, though purple, crimson and white were also worn. Blue was used for servants. Blackwork embroidery was widely used as a form of decoration and this was worked on fine linen for sleeves, underskirts, jackets and caps. Large lace collars framed the face with matching cuffs around the wrists. Initially these were made in Reticella needlelace, but later, plaited bobbin lace was introduced. Bobbin lace patterns were available in a book called *Le Pompe*, and they copied the needlelace designs. Shoulders were accentuated with rolls of fabric decorated with pearls. Sleeves were lavish, and indeed two sets can be seen in many portraits. One set was in blackwork covered with a filmy gauze. A second set, known as false sleeves, hung from the shoulder.

Bodices were tight fitting with a pointed waist at the front and were worn over wide skirts split at the front to reveal an embroidered underskirt. Underneath would have been a tight corset with a wooden busk at the front to keep the stomach flat. A padded roll was tied round the waist to hold out the skirts. It was known as a 'bum roll'. Underwear consisted of chemise, petticoat, silk stockings and garters. Hair was braided at the back into a flat bun and the front hair was brushed over pads of horse hair. A wired, heart-shaped head-dress holding a pearl drop on the forehead completed the picture. Accessories consisted of numerous necklaces and a stick fan of ostrich feathers.

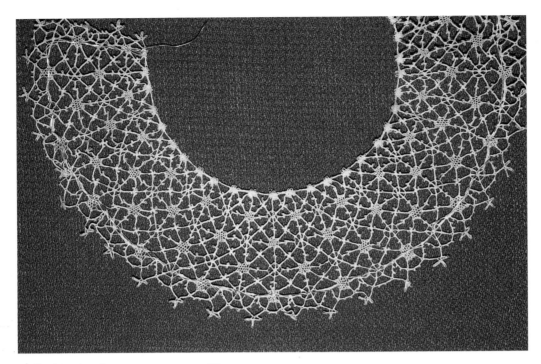

Collar (Fig. 3 and see instructions page 13)

Detail of blackwork sleeve (Fig. 2 and see instructions on page 12)

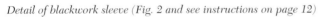

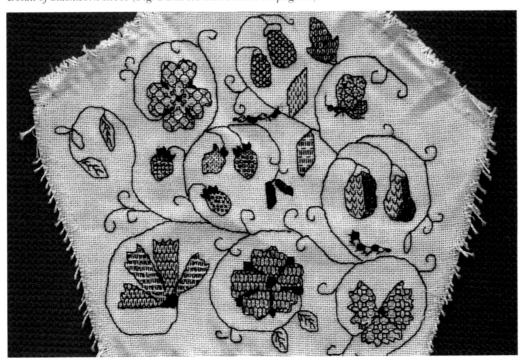

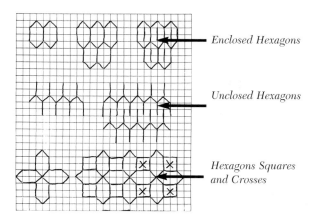

Enclosed Hexagons

Unclosed Hexagons

Hexagons Squares
and Crosses

Hexagons and Crosses

Spaced Squares

Squares and Crosses

Spaced Squares
and Large Crosses

Fig. 1
Blackwork stitch formations

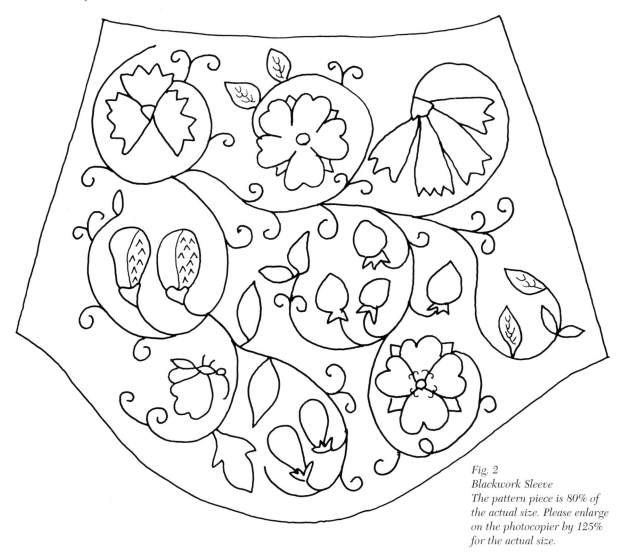

Fig. 2
Blackwork Sleeve
*The pattern piece is 80% of
the actual size. Please enlarge
on the photocopier by 125%
for the actual size.*

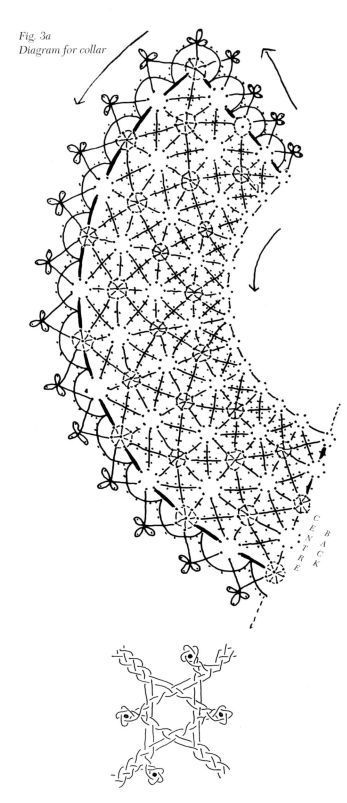

Fig. 3a
Diagram for collar

Fig. 3b
Crossing with four dots (see collar instructions)

Blackwork Sleeve

Blackwork is a form of counted thread embroidery and it needs an even weave fabric in white or cream. Tudor blackwork designs usually included Tudor roses, strawberries, potato flowers and various insects. They were worked in black with touches of gold or red.

Method

1. Trace the sleeve on to firm tracing paper and transfer to some fine even weave fabric.

2. Use a 4B pencil for the tracing, then reverse the design and place it on the fabric. Draw round the design again, pressing hard, and the design will be transferred.

3. Redefine the lines and backstitch the whole outline with one thread of stranded cotton worked over two threads.

4. Fill each area with blackwork patterns using black and some gold. The stitches shown are worked over one or two threads and form hexagons or squares.

5. The crosses can be worked in gold. Use simple running stitches or random stitches to fill the small areas, and feather stitches for the leaf veins.

6. Finish the bottom of the sleeve with close blanket stitch in black and gather just above to fit the arm.

7. Attach a gauze sleeve of the same size at the same time as the gathering thread, fit the two parts together and sew as one.

Collar

40 pairs 100 Brok

Method

Following Fig. 3a, begin at **A** and work a half-stitch circle adding pairs as indicated. The second and third loops at **B** are made with sewings and picots are worked on each plait. Make windmill crossings at **C** and at all plait crossings marked with one dot. At crossings with four dots work as in Fig. 3b. Make the wheel at **D** by adding a further two pairs; you now have six pairs at this point. Divide these so that two pairs plait on either side to form the rim and two pairs plait to the

centre. Make a crossing with the rim pair and the pair coming from the outer edge and plait to the centre. At the crossing add four pairs, and plait these to form the other spokes of the wheel. Make crossings where they meet the rim and bring the rim pairs together to form a four-pair plait at **F**. Continue to add pairs as indicated and continue the outer edge to **G**. Add two pairs at **G** and divide as before. Add two pairs at **H** and plait to the rim. Make crossings with the rim pairs and a six-plait crossing at the centre of the wheel. There will be six pairs at **J**.

All the pairs for the collar are now in place. The half-stitch circles and the wheels alternate and the thick plait at the outer edge will alternate from a six plait to a four plait as the plait at **K** travels down to the neckline and returns on the next row. The neck edge will therefore also have an alternating six and four plait. From now on the outer rim of the wheels will have only one pair on either side. Twist it three times before crossing it with an incoming plait.

When the collar is complete, turn the pattern so that you finish off in reverse of the beginning. Tie and cut off the threads as they accumulate. Oversew fine wire to the outer edge of the collar on the heavy plaits. Make the cuffs by working nine repeats of the pattern.

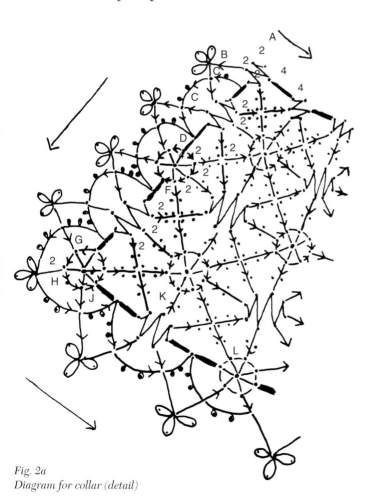

Fig. 2a
Diagram for collar (detail)

The Georgians

Georgian dress was still very ornate and there were many more richly patterned fabrics available, including brocades, silks, satins, and velvets. Pale colours were worn by the ladies and deeper colours by the men. The French court was very influential in fashion, with the rest of Europe endeavouring to follow their lead. Marie Antoinette, for example, introduced the shepherdess style after copying it from French farmers' wives. They looped skirts up into panniers to keep them out of the dirt and tied a flat straw hat on their heads. The court dress version was made in rich materials trimmed with lace and the hat was decorated with flowers and lace. Marie wore this style when she played at the farm Le Hameau at Versailles and it quickly became popular all over Europe. It can be seen in many paintings by Watteau, the eighteenth-century French painter. Chemises and tight corsets were worn, pushing up the bust to be revealed at the low neckline. Sleeves were tight fitting to the elbow where they frothed out in lace ruffles, deeper at the back than the front. Striped material was popular and the stripes always ran round the sleeve rather than down as we would cut them now. In cold weather, quilting was used and it appeared in petticoats, jackets and caps. Hair was brushed back to fall as ringlets at the back.

Men wore pleated coats with numerous buttons and buttonholes on coats, cuffs and pockets, but the coats were rarely fastened at the front or at the back. The coat was worn over knee breeches and a long waistcoat which buttoned at the front but was laced at the back. Corsets were often worn to slim the figure. Underneath was a shirt of linen or silk with a lace jabot at the neck and lace ruffles that hung over the hands. Their hair was carefully rolled back from the forehead, with three rolls at the side. At the back, the hair was tied with black ribbon and placed in a small black bag. The ribbon fastened round the neck to tie at the front, keeping the hair close in to the base of the neck. A false bow was then attached to the bag at the back. The procedure was known as the Solitaire.

Georgian jabot (see instructions, page 16)

Georgian gentleman in jabot and ruffles (Figs. 4 and 5, pattern Fig. 74 and see instructions on page 16)

Jabot

26 pairs 80 Brok, 4 pairs gimp
30 DMC

Method

Hang on pairs as indicated in Fig. 4a.
Add two pairs of gimp at **A**, and another
pair at **B** and carry it in the edge from **C**
to **D**. Add another pair of gimp at **E** and
cut out at **F**, and another pair at **G**
which continues the berries at **H**. Work
the leaves in half stitch and the berries
as honeycomb rings with a tally to the
centre. On each repeat use the gimp
from the berries at **J** to start the leaf and
add another gimp pair at **K**. Make a 23
cm (9 in) length for the jabot and 2 x 18
cm (2 x 7 in) lengths for the sleeves.

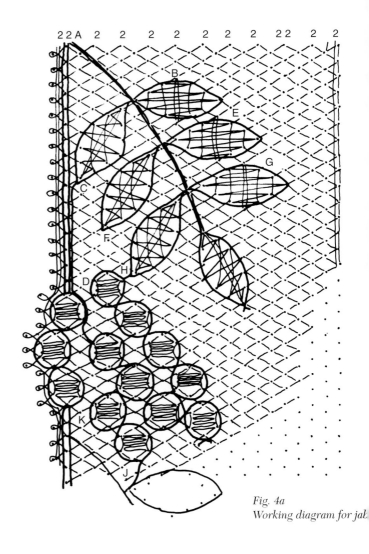

Fig. 4a
Working diagram for jab

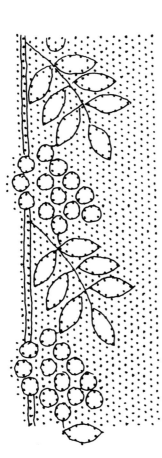

Fig. 4
Pricking for jabot

Butterfly Ruffles

Method (small ruffle)

25 pairs 100 Brok, 2 pairs gimp 30 DMC

Start with three pairs at **A** and add pairs as
false picots from **A** to **B**. Add more pairs as
needed from **C** to **D** and work butterflies as
in Fig. 5a.

16

Method (large ruffle)

42 pairs 100, 2 pairs gimp

Work this as with the small ruffle, but note there are more butterflies and a deeper ground. Follow Fig. 5a and add pairs as false picots when they are required until all pairs are on at **E**. Decrease by taking pairs out as they accumulate on the outer edge from **E** to **F**.

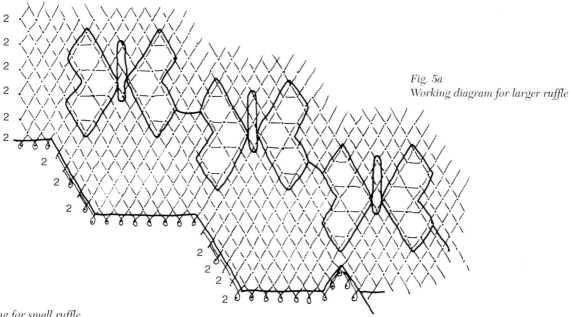

Fig. 5a
Working diagram for larger ruffle

Fig. 5
Pricking for small ruffle

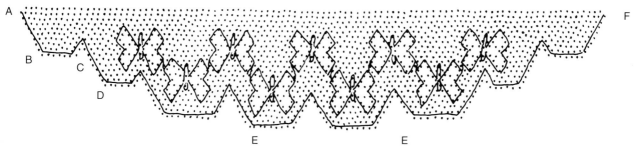

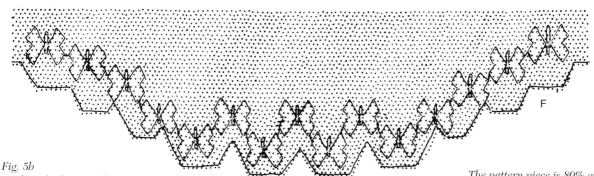

Fig. 5b
Pricking for large ruffle

The pattern piece is 80% of the actual size. Please enlarge on the photocopier by 125% for the actual size.

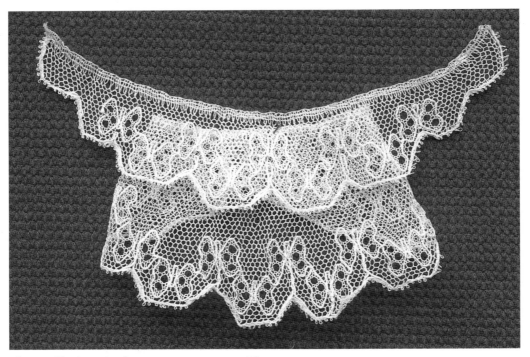

Sleeve ruffles (Fig. 5 and see instructions on page 17)

*Detail of quilted petticoat
worn by Georgian doll (Fig. 6 and
see instructions on page 20)*

Back view of doll in Georgian costume
(Pattern Fig. 73 and see instructions for trimmings on pages 17 and 20)

Quilted Petticoat for Georgian Doll

Use silk satin and blanket or wadding measuring 48 cm (19 in) by the required length.

Method

Trace the design on to firm tracing paper with a 4B pencil. Reverse the paper and trace the design repeat on to thin wadding or blanket. Define the outline. Four repeats make a 46 cm (18 in) petticoat. Tack the silk firmly to the blanket and put into an embroidery frame. Make small, even stab stitches through both materials, following the design on the wrong side and checking frequently that the stitches are even on the right side. When complete, make a seam at the back and a small hem at the top and bottom. Run a narrow ribbon or cord through the hem at the top and gather to fit the doll's waist.

Regency

Dress became simpler in this period. By 1800, tight corsets were gone and dress waistlines had moved up to be positioned just under the breasts, providing a long, lean silhouette. Thin, gauzy material was used, and the hair was piled up and decorated with ribbons which gave a Grecian neoclassical look. The fine muslin clung to the figure, and with small sleeves and a low neckline it was very revealing. In some cases in the northern cold climates this fashion caused some young girls to die of pneumonia. The slim line demanded a narrow petticoat and as this still revealed the legs pantaloons were worn. They were copied from male breeches but for convenience were made as two separate legs which tied round

.Fig. 6
Pattern for quilting

the waist. These, as well as the dresses, were soon being decorated with lace and embroidery. The lace of this period was light and open. By this time, net was made by machine which created a new industry of needlerun net and appliquéd motifs. Lace of this sort was cheaper so that many more people could afford to wear it. A small jacket called a Spencer was popular; it had a high neck with a puffed upper sleeve. Kashmir shawls were fashionable and the richly woven borders contrasted with the pale, high-waisted dresses. Bonnets were high-crowned to accommodate the hairstyle and were placed over the small lace caps that were worn indoors.

By 1825, coloured silks and patterned materials began to appear and the waistline began to descend slightly, though it was still well above the waist. Skirts were ankle-length in a bell shape with the hemline accentuated with ruching and lace. There was also increased fullness in the sleeve with frills of lace and often extra padding. Necklines were low, and often worn off-the-shoulder in the evening. Petticoats had extra frills to hold the shape of the skirt and tight corsets were once again in vogue. Pantaloons were still worn, though with more lace and embroidery than before, and accompanied by silk stockings and soft, flat shoes with strappings rather like our ballet shoes. This era was often referred to as the 'Romantic Period'.

Dress in Carrickmacross 1805

30 DMC thread couched with 100 Brok.

Use cotton net with cotton organdie; silk tulle with silk organza; nylon net with nylon organza.

Method

1. Trace the design on tracing paper with a fairly thick pen so that it can be seen clearly through the net and organdie. Trace the edge design to fit the base of the centre panel, repeating it to make a 58 cm (23 in) length.

2. Cover with plastic film.

3. Place net over the design, positioning it with the panel to the centre, and tack to the paper.

4. Place organdie over the net and tack firmly to the paper. Work tacking stitches in-between the design to hold it firmly while working.

5. With fine stitches 1 mm apart, oversew a single thread of 30 DMC round the design with the 100 Brok. **Do not stitch through the paper, only through the net and organdie.** Try to make a continuous flow – the thread can be doubled back at dead ends. Finish off the oversewing thread with a few back stitches and start a new thread in the same way.

6. When the design is complete, take out the tacking threads and remove the paper.

7. Finish the outer scalloped edge of the design with close buttonhole stitch.

8. Carefully cut away the organdie round the design to reveal the net. Cut back to the buttonholed edge.

9. Sew the back seam and gather the top. Make an underskirt 41cm (16 in) wide by length to ankle, gather to fit the doll and attach the net, adjusting the net gathers towards the back.

Doll in Regency costume, 1805
(For dress and spencer pattern see Figs. 7 and 75 and instructions on pages 21 and 102)

Close-up of front of Carrickmacross dress, worn under Regency 1805 dress shown on page 22 (Fig. 7 and see instructions on page 21)

Fig. 7
Carrickmacross dress
The pattern piece is 80% of the actual
size. Please enlarge on the photocopier
by 125% for the actual size.

Regency Dress Edge 1820

24 pairs 100 Brok, single gimp 30 DMC

Method

Set up as indicated in Fig. 8a. The outer shell edge is worked independently of the main pattern. Joining occurs when the gimp meets the edge at **B** and when the weavers meet and return at **A**.

Make blocks of rose ground and tallies and work point ground in the net area. Work the diamond in half stitch. Work picots from **G** to **B**.

Pairs will accumulate from **G** to **A**; keep them bunched together even inside the diamond. Take the second or third pair of the bunch to work the picots from **A** to **B**. Work the outer shell edge in cloth and twist, taking two pairs out to form a plait and picot at **C**.

Make a 61 cm (24 in) length and join into a circle with sewings or the overlaid method. Make a 28 cm (11 in) length of the outer shell edge for the dress neckline.

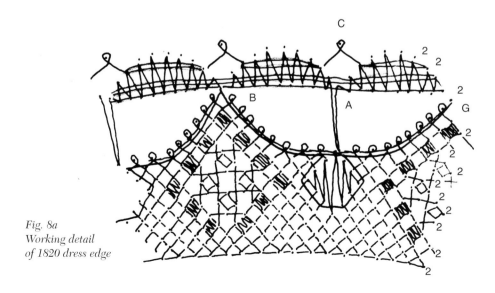

Fig. 8
Pricking for 1820 dress edge

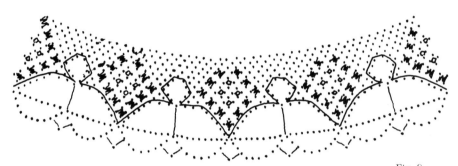

Fig. 8a
Working detail
of 1820 dress edge

Doll in Regency costume, 1820, featuring dress edge, sleeve frill, and stole
(Figs. 8, 9 and 10, pattern Fig. 76 and see instructions on pages 25, 28 and 29)

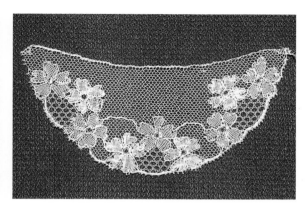

Dress edge, 1820 (Fig. 8 and see instructions on page 28)

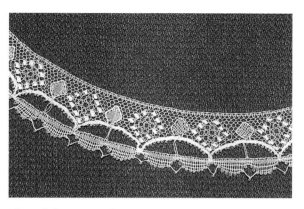

Sleeve frill (Fig. 9 and see instructions on page 25)

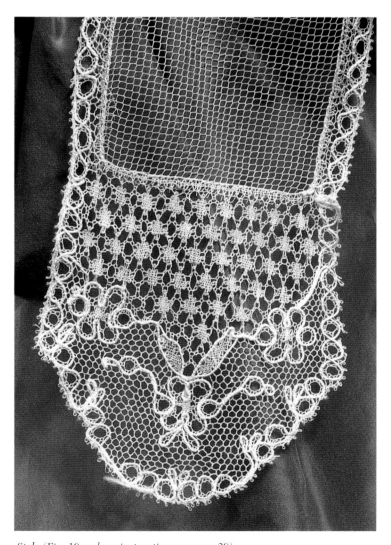

Stole (Fig. 10 and see instructions on page 29)

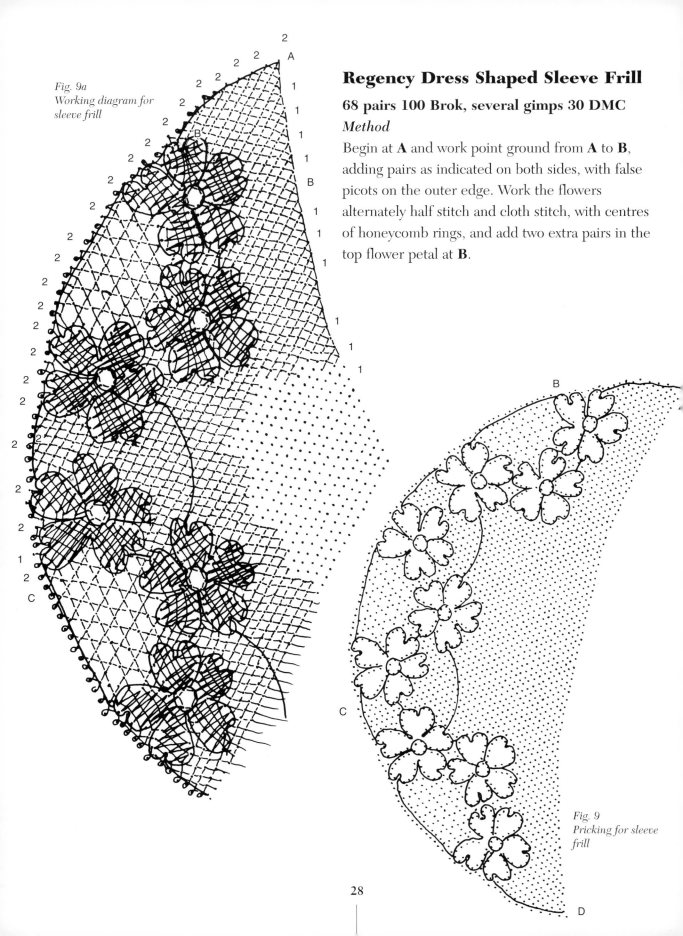

Fig. 9a
Working diagram for sleeve frill

Regency Dress Shaped Sleeve Frill

68 pairs 100 Brok, several gimps 30 DMC
Method

Begin at **A** and work point ground from **A** to **B**, adding pairs as indicated on both sides, with false picots on the outer edge. Work the flowers alternately half stitch and cloth stitch, with centres of honeycomb rings, and add two extra pairs in the top flower petal at **B**.

Fig. 9
Pricking for sleeve frill

Two gimps are needed in each flower; they carry over as indicated wherever possible or are cut out at **X**. Continue to add pairs when necessary on the outer edge from **B** to **C**, taking them out as they accumulate from **C** to the end at **D**.

Regency Dress Stole

54 pairs 100 Brok, several pairs of gimp 30 DMC

This has two tie ends attached to net with a pea edge continuing along the net edge for the required length.

Method

Start at **A**, adding pairs as false picots from **A** to **B**, and adding pairs from **A** to **C** as you need them. Work point ground on the outer part and honeycomb with mayflowers in the inner part. Pairs will accumulate from **D** to **E**. Gradually take these out, leaving eight pairs at the end to work the edging from **E**.

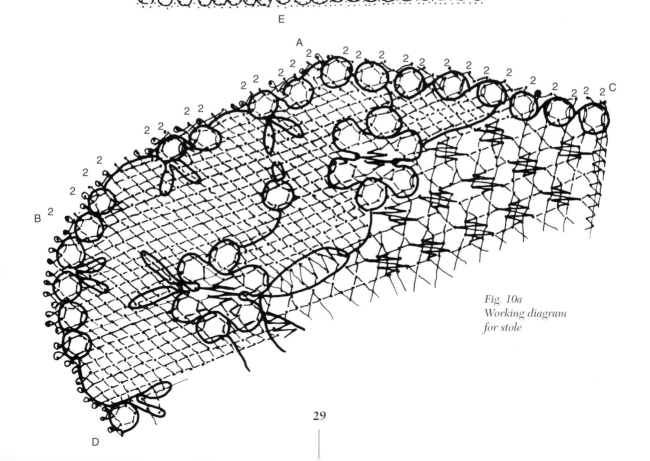

Fig. 10
Pricking for stole

Fig. 10a
Working diagram for stole

The Victorians

This was the age of wealthy new industrialists whose wives and daughters exploited these riches with extravagant attire. There were no shops or stores in which to buy off-the-peg clothes until the twentieth century, so fabrics and trimmings had to be bought at a draper's and taken to a dressmaker to make up. The design would be copied from colour fashion plates, usually taken from French books, and the dress would be ready in several days or sometimes weeks. The sewing machine was not invented until 1860 and was then not in wide use until the 1880s, so everything was hand sewn. Hats were often made or trimmed to match the outfit. Ladies would have dresses for all occasions and would change them six or seven times a day. They chose a light dress for the mornings for breakfast and writing letters, a more formal dress for visiting or shopping, a decorative dress for promenading in the park, another for taking tea with friends and yet another one or two for evening dinner parties, theatre trips or dances.

Throughout the nineteenth century it was unthinkable to wear sleeveless dresses in the daytime, reveal one's ankles at any time, or go out without a hat or bonnet. Lace and ribbon caps were worn indoors, but these gradually disappeared for unmarried women. Lace-trimmed chemises and tight-boned corsets were worn, while pantaloons gradually moved to knee-length, but they retained two separate legs until the twentieth century.

Close-up of edge and inset on pantaloons (Figs. 11 and 11a, pattern Fig. 71 and see instructions on page 32)

Throughout the century a variety of styles emerged, developed, became extreme and then gave way to others, always focusing on one or other part of the anatomy. Each fashionable shape could not exist without the essential substructure, tight corsets, crinolines, bustles, bum rolls or sleeve pads. Tiny waists were accentuated by very full skirts, often tiered for extra width, with numerous petticoats to hold them out. Jacket bodices were popular, with a half chemise tied round the waist and undersleeves tied round the upper arm; these were the only parts that could be laundered. The crinoline was invented in 1856 to dispense with the petticoats and yet still retain the triangular shape. It was lighter than a petticoat, being formed of steel, whalebone or cane hoops held together by tapes and tied round the waist, and only one fancy petticoat was needed. By the time it reached its extreme, over two metres wide, it became the butt of cartoonists. Because it was cheap, it was worn by all classes, even factory workers. It must have been both inconvenient and tricky to manage.

The crinoline width gradually gave way to the bustle, a half-hooped structure tied at the back with skirts draped over it. This also reached extremes until it too disappeared in the 1890s. Hats and bonnets were small, hair was parted in the middle to fall in ringlets at the back, and lappets were still worn in the evening as was a triangular headscarf called a fascinator.

Victorian costume with crinoline.
(Pattern Fig. 77 and see instructions on page 32)

Close-up of jacket edge worn by Victorian doll
(Fig. 12 and see instructions on page 32)

Edge and Inset of Pantaloons for Crinoline Doll (1860)

14 pairs 100 Brok

Method

Set up pairs as shown and work Torchon ground with cloth stitch hearts. Work cloth and twist on the fan edge with two twists on the outer edge.

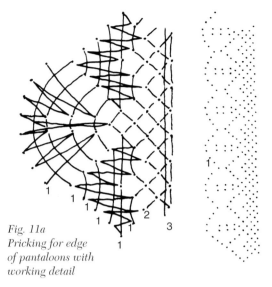

Fig. 11a
Pricking for edge of pantaloons with working detail

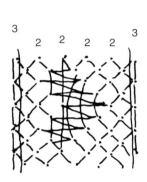

Fig. 11
Pricking for inset of pantaloons with working detail

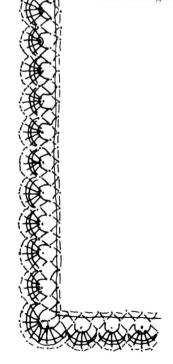

Fig. 12
Pricking for jacket edge

Jacket Edge for Crinoline Doll

9 pairs 50 DMC

Method

Start at the back of the neck and work 18 cm (7 in) to the corner, approx 36 cm (14 in) to the next corner, and 18 cm (7 in) to meet at the back of the neck. Work the shell edge with cloth and twist, using the pivot pin several times, taking the weaving pair round the pin and under the pair on the pivot pin (this makes a tidier finish).

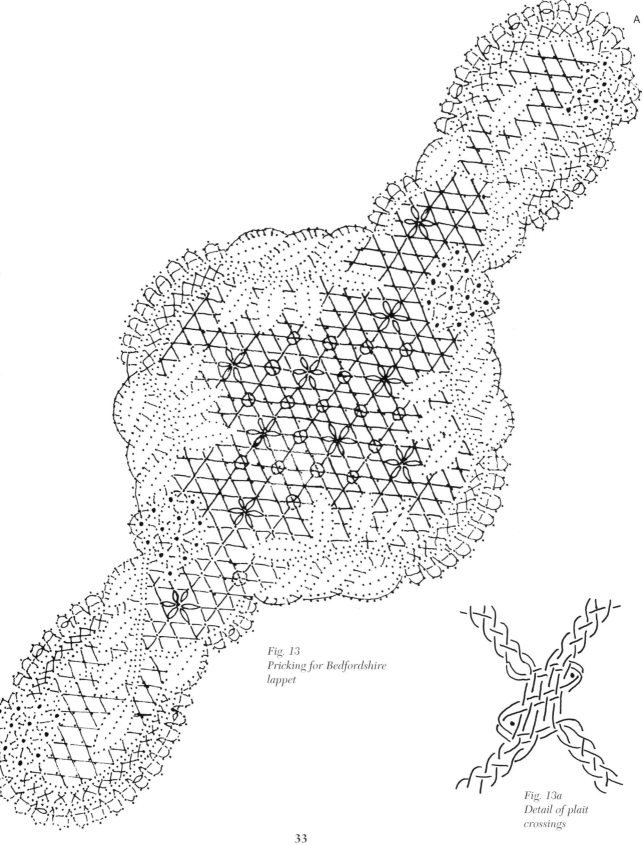

A

Fig. 13
Pricking for Bedfordshire
lappet

Fig. 13a
Detail of plait
crossings

Lappet (Fig. 13 and see instructions below)

Lappet for Crinoline Doll

84 pairs approx at the widest part 100 Brok

This is a Thomas Lester type lappet worked in Bedfordshire lace. It is not easy and should not be attempted by those unfamiliar with Bedfordshire techniques.

Method

Begin at A. Start the ninepin edge and small trails with crossed plaits in-between. Work the berries in cloth stitch blocks with a raised tally in each. Work the plaited ground with crossings as in Fig. 13a and make the wheels by separating the plait and taking one pair twisted on either side. Bring the plaited pairs through these and make a windmill crossing in the centre.

Work the leaves in cloth stitch with a twist to form the veins. Make picots on the outer edge. Pairs will increase over the head on either side. Add these as you need them and take them out when they accumulate in the trails and leaves. Fasten off as neatly as possible at the finish.

Fascinator (Fig. 14 and see instructions below)

Fascinator

85 pairs approx silk thread equivalent to 50 DMC, several gimps 30 DMC

This is worked in point ground and really needs working experience of Floral Bucks.

Method

Start at **A** with the centre flower. Add pairs as necessary to complete the flower and leave out pairs for the ground. Add pairs as false picots on either side for the honeycomb ring edge. Work from **A** to **B** and **A** to **C** simultaneously, adding pairs as required and working from one side to the other. Work the edge in cloth stitch trails with a foot side and a gimp at the edge.

Pairs will accumulate at **C**; take them out and continue down to E. Work the inner flowers in cloth stitch as in Fig. 14a and make gimp fingers for leaves. Work the outer leaves to **E** in half stitch. When the centre is complete, make the two lappet ends. Sew in approx 40 pairs from **B** to **C** and work down to **F**. Reverse the pattern for the lappet end to work the other side.

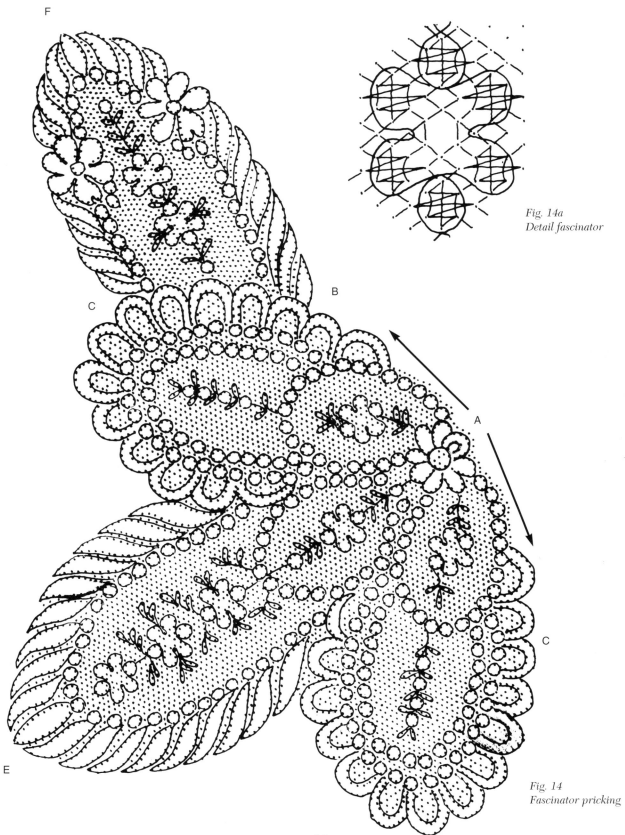

F

C

B

A

C

E

Fig. 14a
Detail fascinator

Fig. 14
Fascinator pricking

Lace for doll with Bustle (1875)

This is an evening dress, so choose a doll with a good shoulder and neckline and arms that can take short sleeves.

Method (Roses)

12 pairs Guttermans silk 100/3

Work the strip, starting at **A** and working alternate cloth and half-stitch petals, making a foot on both sides. Take out pairs as they accumulate and tie off the rest as a bunch at the end. Trim and carefully roll the strip from small end to large, gathering slightly and stitching, forming rose petals as you proceed. These can be tightly closed or open to make them realistic.

Method (Leaf)

8 pairs Guttermans silk 100/3

Start at the tip with five pairs. Make a foot on either side and add pairs on either side. Form a vein by twisting the weaver and tie off as a bunch at the end. Place these under the roses and sew into place on the neckline, sides, and at the back.

Fig. 15
Pricking for roses and leaf

Victorian evening dress with bustle and roses
(Fig. 15, pattern: Fig. 78 and see instructions on pages 37 and 39)

Rose (Fig. 15 and see instructions on page 37)

Fan (Fig. 16 and see instructions on page 39)

Method (Fan)

49 pairs black 80 Cotona, several pairs of pink and green

Start at **A,** adding pairs as indicated. Work the braid from **A** to **B** leaving two pairs out at each inner pinhole. Add a green pair at **C,** removing it at **X** each time, and another at **D** which carries on through. Run the green pair up and down the lower fan to form the stalk.

Work each petal in pink, adding where necessary and taking out at **X**. Add a pink pair to edge the outer shell edge. Follow the diagram and finish with a narrow braid as in the beginning, taking pairs out as they accumulate. This final braid is hidden under the fan's stick.

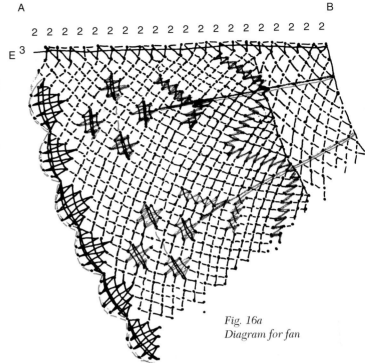

Fig. 16a
Diagram for fan

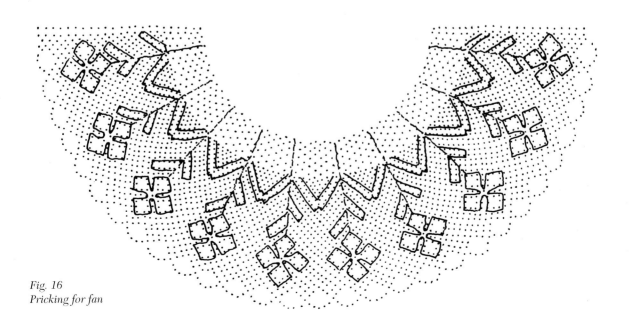

Fig. 16
Pricking for fan

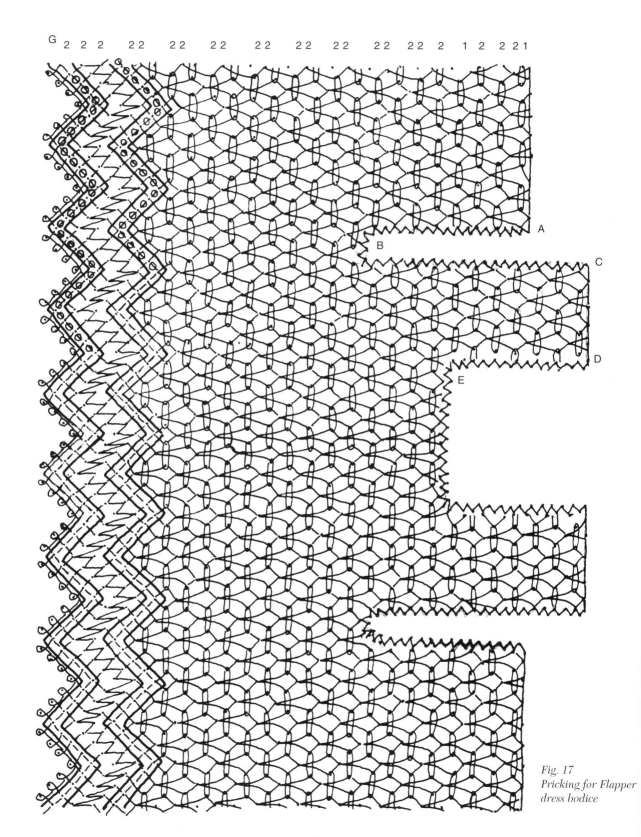

Fig. 17
Pricking for Flapper
dress bodice

Flapper Style

In the 1920s, female fashion changed dramatically. Women's hemlines rose to knee level and their hair was cut short into a bob. The styles made them seem bosomless, waistless and hipless and with dresses often without form, shaping or fastening and identical back and front.

Flapper Dress

32 pairs black 30 DMC for the skirt, 52 pairs for the bodice, 2 pairs black perlé 12, 2 pairs red 30 DMC

The dress is in three parts: a skirt made in a strip, a bodice with armholes and square neck, and small strip sleeves. The dress should be sleeveless, but without a porcelain doll, the arms will not come up to the shoulders, so adjust the sleeve strip to fit. Triangular ground is used throughout with a coloured border and added beads. Cut out the bodice shape with a paper towel as a pattern and try it on the doll for size. Use this pattern for the petticoat plus 7 cm (3 in).

Method (Bodice)

Start at the centre back. Add pairs as indicated in Fig. 17 and work triangular ground with a picot border. Sew in beads as you progress with a crochet hook. Carry the pairs in a cloth stitch trail from **A** to **B** and drop them out again and add others from **B** to **C**. Carry the pairs again on the neckline **D** to **E** and leave out on the opposite side. Work the other armhole in the same way, taking pairs out when no longer required. Finish at centre back and join, leaving a small back neck opening. Join shoulders.

Method (Skirt)

Make five repeats of the pattern to form sixteen points and join into a circle as neatly as possible (See Fig. 17d)

Method (Sleeves)

Make two and join each into a circle. It may be necessary to add more triangular ground if the doll's arms are short. Fit these into the armholes (See Fig. 17a).

Fig. 17a Pricking for Flapper dress sleeve

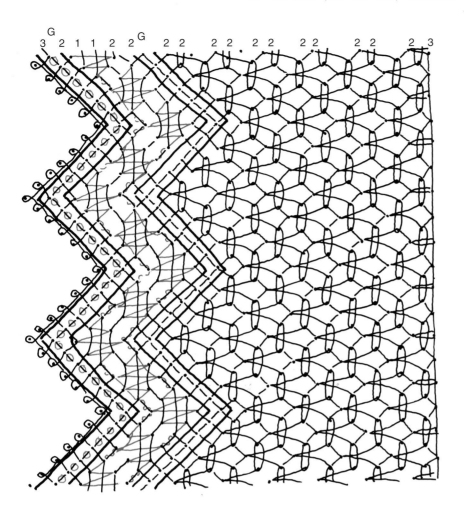

Fig. 17b
Inserting beads
with sewings

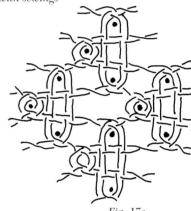

Fig. 17c
Detail of
triangular ground

Fig. 17d
Pricking for Flapper dress skirt

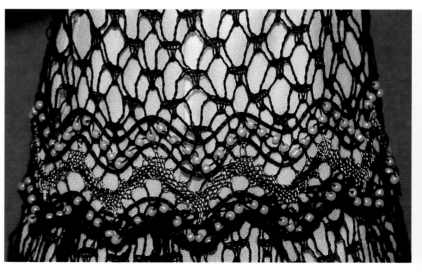

Close-up of Flapper, showing triangular ground
(Fig. 17c and see instructions on page 41)

Doll dressed in the Flapper Dress, 1920
(Figs. 17a, b, c, d and instructions on page 41)

CHAPTER TWO
⅟₁₂ SCALE DOLLS

The miniature residents in a dolls' house give life to a room setting. They can be set in any period in history, but their clothes and the furnishings must be appropriate for the period portrayed, and this includes the lace. I have provided patterns here for edges and insets, collars, fans, and shawls etc., suitable for clothing and furnishings for a mid-Victorian period. Suitable dolls range from grannies to babies.

Dressing ⅟₁₂ scale dolls is more intricate than the 46 cm (18 in) size. Doll-making kits are available which are based around pipe cleaners, allowing the dolls to be moved into poses, but they are delicate and will eventually break with too much undressing so the clothes are usually sewn on to the doll. It is possible to obtain miniature all-porcelain dolls which can be undressed, but they are obviously not flexible. Choose soft materials for the clothes, and use Bondaweb and Fraycheck to eliminate hems. Attach all the trimmings to the dress before making up and fitting chemises and pantaloons. Make the skirt and gather to fit before attaching it to the doll. Make the bodice and fit it to the doll and finally attach the sleeves. It is better to attach the hair on to the doll after dressing so that it does not ruffle.

Lace patterns in bobbin lace, worked in fine thread, have their difficulties however easy the pattern. One cannot see the design in progress because of the forest of pins, so use the finest available. Point ground (half stitch, three twists, pin) gives a softer lace whereas Torchon (cloth stitch, pin, cloth stitch, twist) is firmer. Some of the patterns are of mixed techniques, for example honeycomb rings and picots with Torchon. This is not traditional, but it does produce an attractive lace.

Edges and Insets

The following edges can be worked in Torchon or in point ground but Torchon gives a much firmer edge. They are suitable for dolls' clothes, tablecloth edges, sheets and pillowcases, bed valances, curtain edges and curtain frills.

Spanish or French fan

6 pairs 100 Brok

This is a traditional pattern but when worked very fine it proves the smallest and easiest edge to work.

Method

Set up as shown – the lines indicate the number of twists required. After the first row of the shell, take the weaver round the pivot pin at **A** and under the last pair worked, then back to the outer edge. This is the principle for most of the edges as it makes a small neat shell.

Shell edge with gimp ring

8 pairs 100 Brok, 1 pair gimp 30 DMC
Method

Set up as shown and work the shell edge as in the previous pattern. Work honeycomb rings with a gimp surround.

Shell edge with matching inset

10 pairs for both
Method

Set up as shown and work shell edge as before with cloth stitch blocks and rose ground.

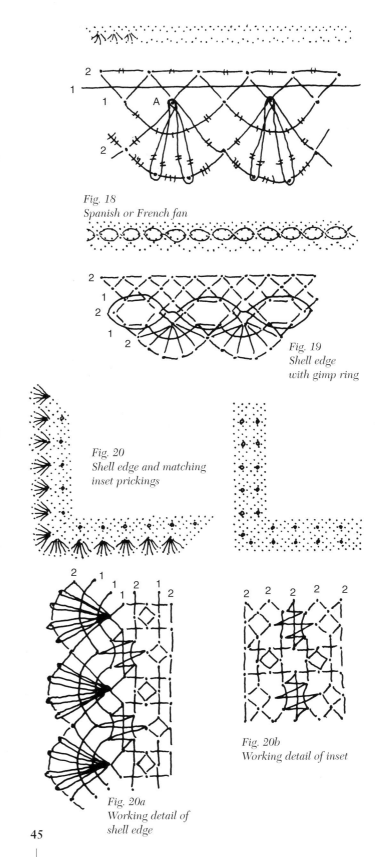

Fig. 18
Spanish or French fan

Fig. 19
*Shell edge
with gimp ring*

Fig. 20
*Shell edge and matching
inset prickings*

Fig. 20b
Working detail of inset

Fig. 20a
*Working detail of
shell edge*

Edges (Figs. 18, 19, 20 and 22 and see instructions on pages 45 and 46)

Fig. 21 Spider edge

Spider Edge

10 pairs 100 Brok

Method

Set up as shown and work Torchon ground with spiders and a cloth stitch trail at the edge. Take out two pairs as shown to make a plait and picot at **A**.

Spider inset

10 pairs 100 Brok

Method

This is a very simple inset worked in Torchon.

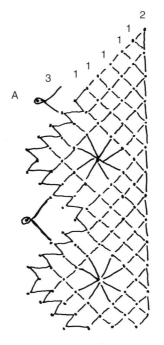

Fig. 21a
Working detail

Fig. 22
Spider inset
pricking

Edges (Fig. 23 and Fig. 60 and see instructions on pages 48 and 85)

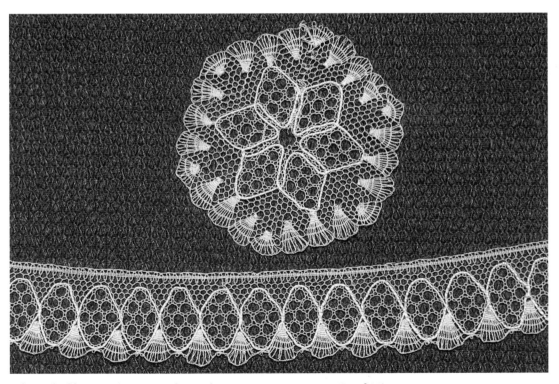

Edge and table centre (Figs. 24 and 56 and see instructions on pages 49 and 81)

Zigzag Rings

24 pairs 100 Brok, 1 pair gimp 30 DMC
Method

Set up as shown and work shell edge
as before using cloth stitch blocks, honeycomb
rings and honeycomb ground.

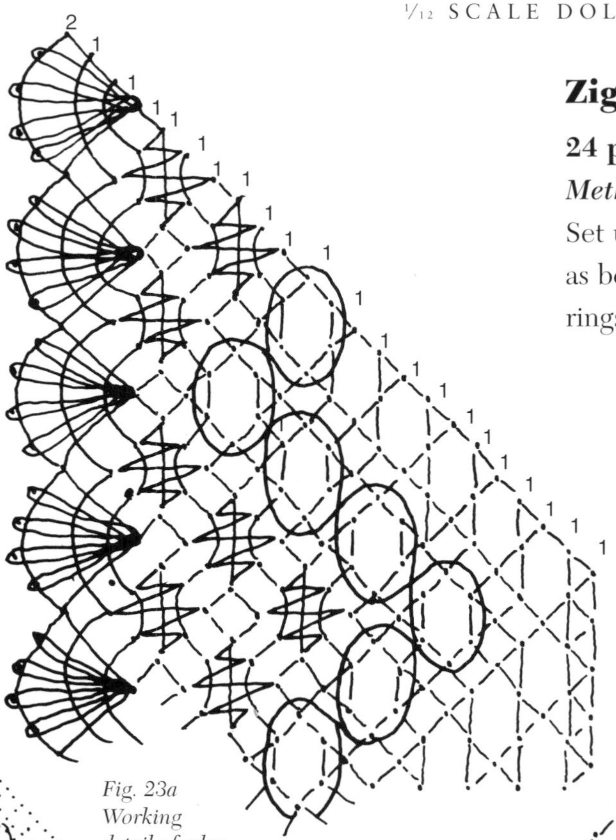

*Fig. 23a
Working
detail of edge*

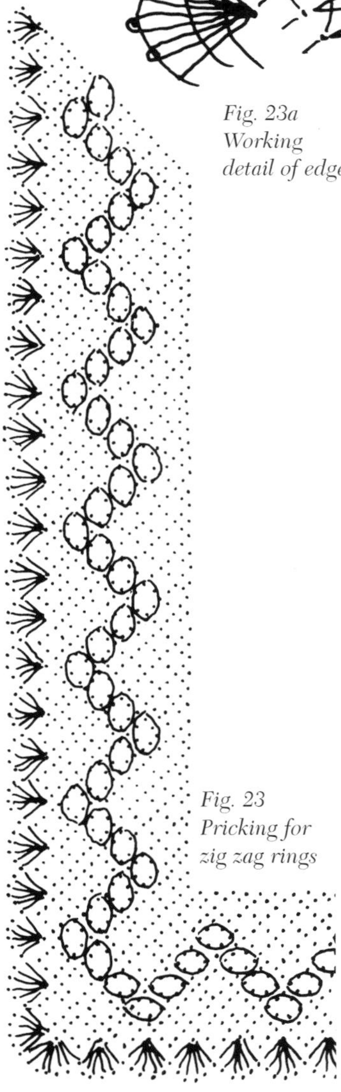

*Fig. 23
Pricking for
zig zag rings*

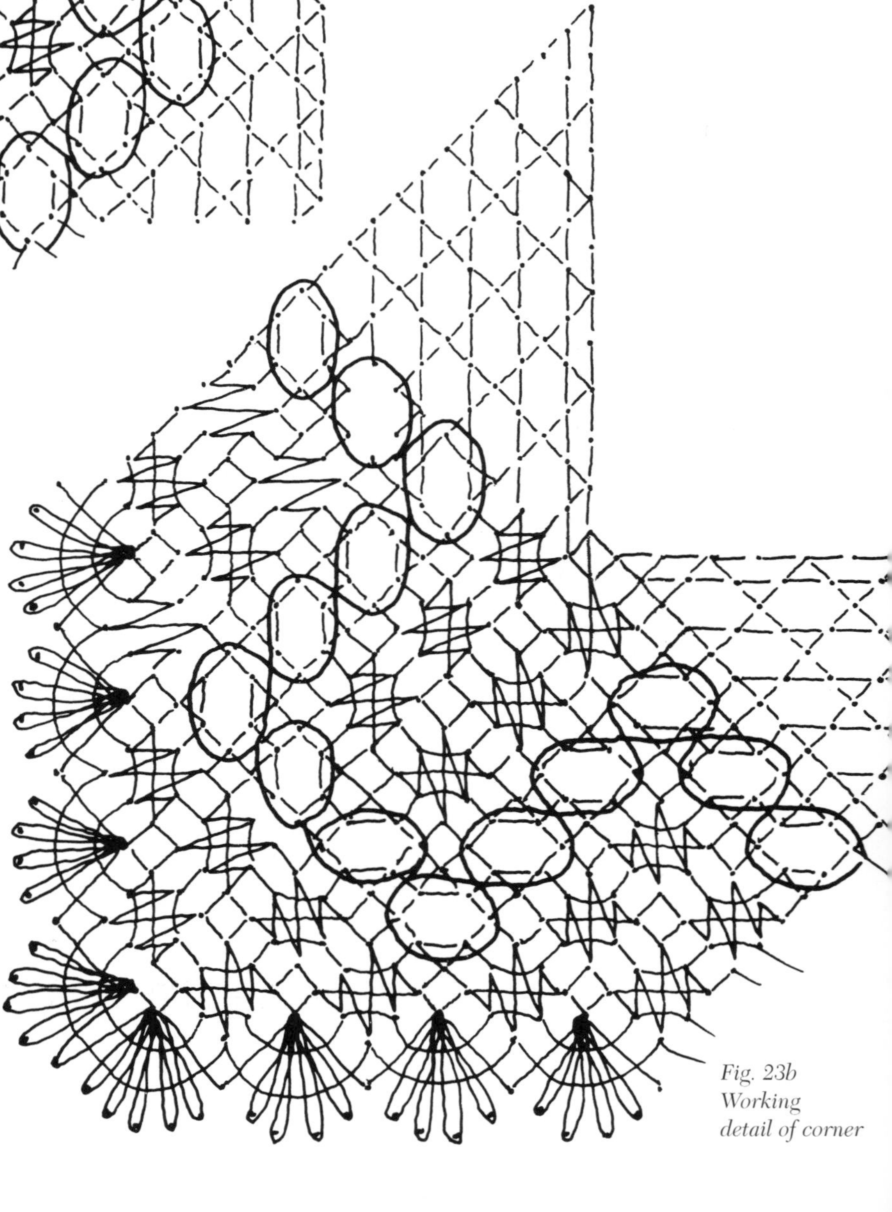

*Fig. 23b
Working
detail of corner*

Honeycomb block and Shell edge

22 pairs 100 Brok,
1 pair gimp 30 DMC

Method

Torchon or point ground can be used. Set up as shown. Work shells as before. Work point ground outside the gimps and honeycomb inside the gimps.

Double Honeycomb with fingers

16 pairs 50 DMC (large) 100 Brok (small) 2 pairs gimp 30 DMC

Method

Set up as shown and work honeycomb rings, taking the gimp out to work the fingers and back in for the next ring. Make picots in point ground.

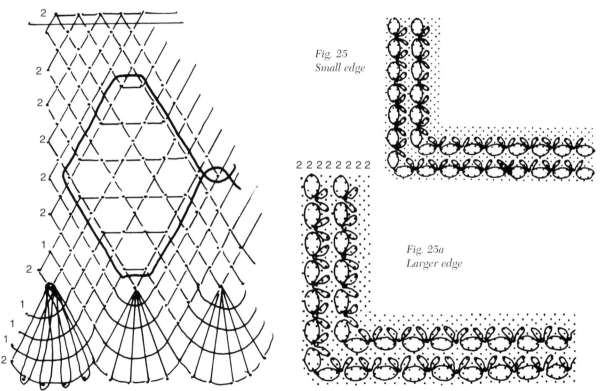

Fig. 25
Small edge

Fig. 25a
Larger edge

Fig. 24a
Working detail for honeycomb block and shell edge

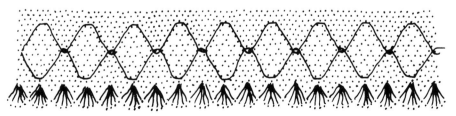

Fig. 24
Honeycomb block and shell edge

Edge on quilt (Fig. 25 and see instructions on page 49)

Bertha collar and edge, and matching collar (see Figs. 29 and 21 and instructions on pages 46 and 53)

Collars and needlelace (Figs. 26, 27, 28, and 50 and see instructions on pages 52, 53 and 73)

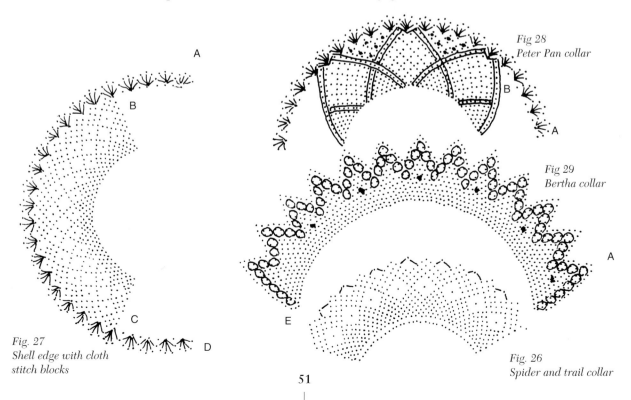

A

B

Fig 28
Peter Pan collar

B

A

Fig 29
Bertha collar

A

E

Fig. 27
Shell edge with cloth
stitch blocks

C

D

Fig. 26
Spider and trail collar

Collars

Spiders and Trails

19 pairs 120 Brok

This collar matches the edge in Fig. 21 and is worked in the same way.

Method

Set up as shown and cloth stitch one pair at **A** through to **B** to form the collar's edge. Work Torchon ground with spiders and a cloth stitch trail at the edge, taking two pairs out to form a picot at **C**. Finish as neatly as possible, taking a pair through and back as at the beginning and darning the threads away.

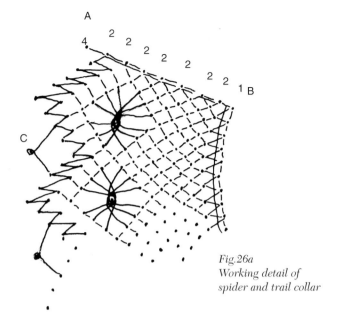

Fig.26a
Working detail of spider and trail collar

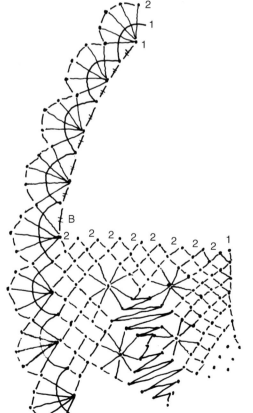

Fig.27a
Working detail of shell edge with cloth stitch blocks

Shell Edge with cloth stitch blocks

21 pairs 120 Brok

Method

Start at **A** with four pairs and work a shell edge to **B**. Start the ground at **B,** adding pairs as shown. Work spiders and cloth stitch blocks, finishing off neatly at **C**. Continue the shell edge to **D** and sew the shells to the collar fronts, tucking the last shell under for neatness.

Point Ground Peter Pan or Bertha

21 pairs 120 Brok, 2 pairs gimp 30 DMC

Method

Start at **A** with four pairs as shown and work the shell edge to **B**. Add pairs as shown through the gimp and work honeycomb stitch inside the gimp. Work the triangles of honeycomb with rose ground on the outer triangle and point ground or Torchon in the inner triangles. Continue to **B** and finish off as neatly as possible. Finish the shell edge and attach both the shell edges to the collar. This pattern can be extended to make a Bertha: use Fig. 28b and work as before.

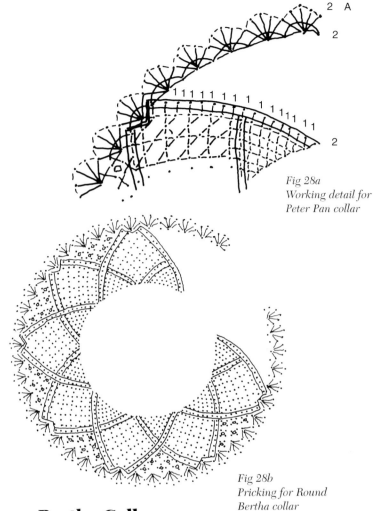

*Fig 28a
Working detail for
Peter Pan collar*

*Fig 28b
Pricking for Round
Bertha collar*

Bertha Collar

18 pairs 120 Brok, 1 pair gimp 30 DMC

This can be worked in Torchon or point ground.

Method

Set up as shown and start at **A**. Work four pin rings as shown, adding pairs as false picots. The pairs will accumulate from **B** to **C**; keep them bunched together and work picots with the second or third pairs of the bunch from **C** to **D** in order to work the next row of rings. Work tallies in alternate points. Finish off with the final row of rings, taking pairs out as they accumulate, and tie off at **E**.

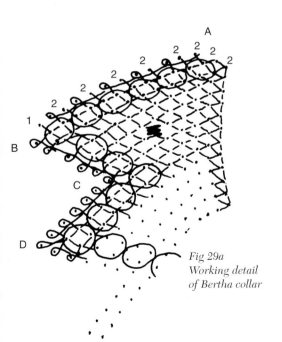

*Fig 29a
Working detail
of Bertha collar*

Plastrons

Point Ground

36 pairs 120 Brok, 3 pairs gimp 30 DMC

Method

Begin at **A** and add pairs as indicated as false picots. Work honeycomb rings on the outer edge and honeycomb rings with gimp fingers down the centre. Divide at the neck front **B** and work the sides to **C**. Remove pairs as they accumulate and finish off as neatly as possible at **C**. The direction of the ground will change at the shoulder line. The larger pricking will fit a 35 to 40 cm (14 to 16 in) doll.

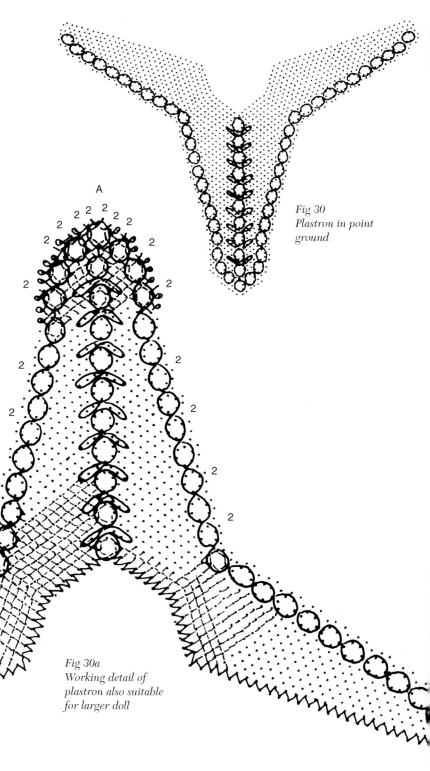

Fig 30
Plastron in point ground

Fig 30a
Working detail of plastron also suitable for larger doll

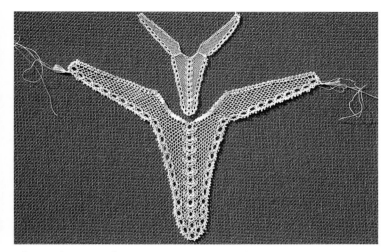

Plastron (Fig. 30 and see instructions on page 54)

The dolls' house lounge with granny and mother in plastrons, and carpet and firescreen in cross stitch
(see instructions for plastrons on pages 54 and 56)

Torchon Plastron

48 pairs 120 Brok, 2 pairs gimp 30 DMC

Method

Begin at **A** and add pairs as indicated on either side as false picots. Add as needed down to **B** and work honeycomb rings with picots on the outer edge and cloth or half-stitch trails with Torchon or rose ground in-between. Work the honeycomb rings from **C** to **D**, taking pairs out as they accumulate on the outer edge. Finish off as neatly as possible at **D**. The larger pricking will fit a 35 to 40 cm (14 to 16 in) doll but the neckline will need enlarging.

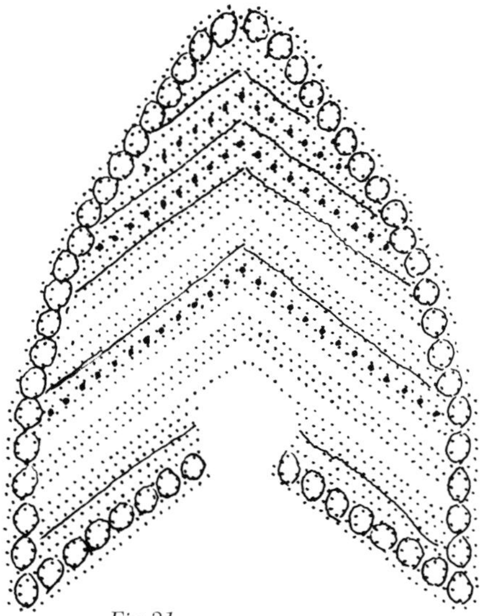

Fig 31
Torchon plastron pricking

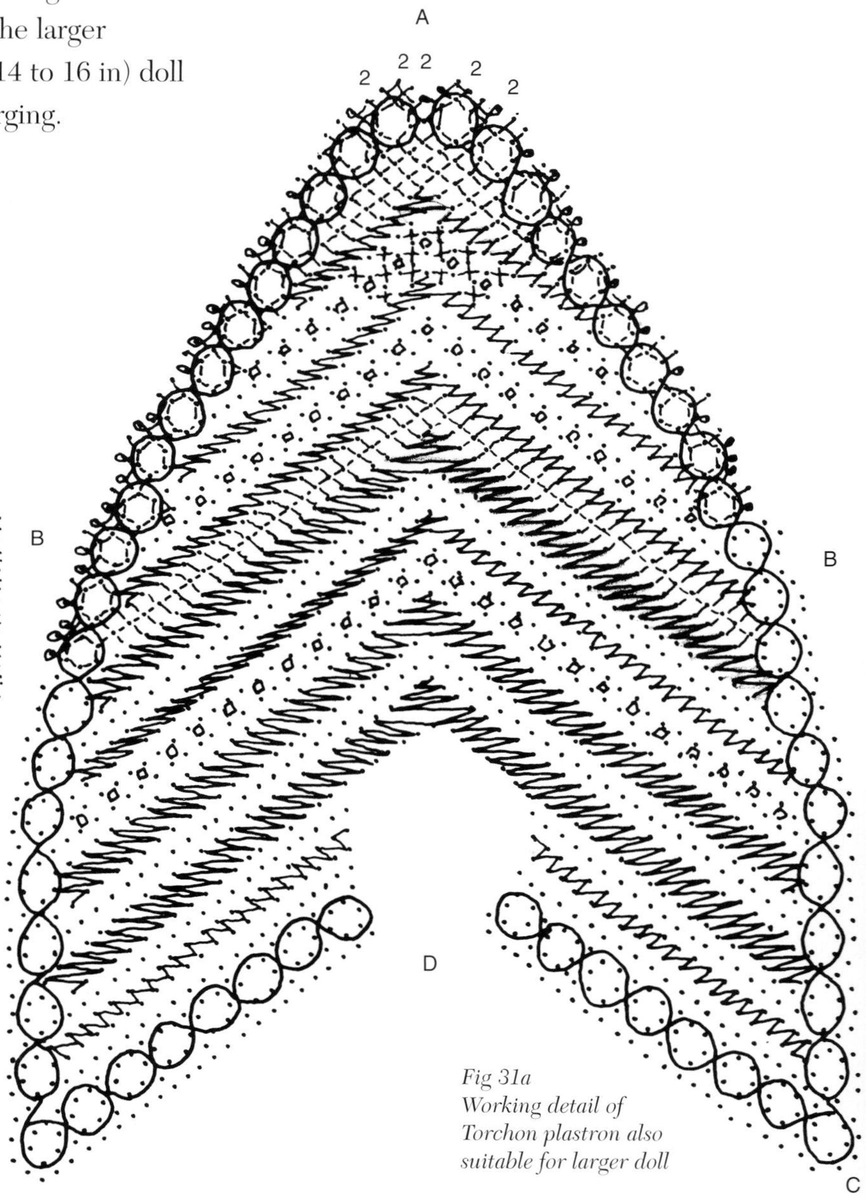

Fig 31a
Working detail of Torchon plastron also suitable for larger doll

Other Miniature Accessories

Lappet

24 pairs 120 Brok 2 pairs gimp 30 DMC for the small size (at the widest part). 24 pairs 50 DMC 2 pairs gimp 12 perlé for the larger size.
Method

Work in point ground. Begin at **A** and add pairs as indicated as false picots on either side. Work cloth stitch blocks and honeycomb rings with picots on the outer edge. Work honeycomb stitch in the cap centre. Finish off as neatly as possible at the end and darn the threads away.

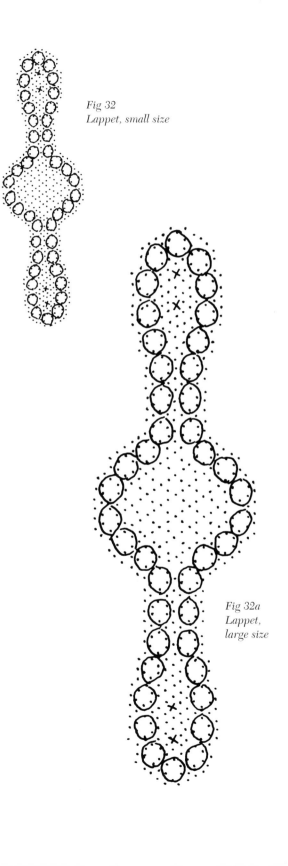

Fig 32
Lappet, small size

Fig 32a
Lappet, large size

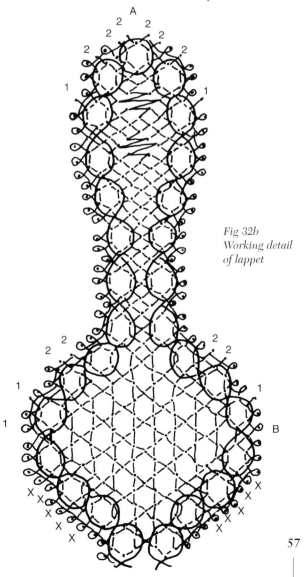

Fig 32b
Working detail of lappet

Granny in plastron and lappet (Figs. 31 and 32 and see instructions on pages 56 and 57)

Fan (Fig. 34 and see instructions on page 61)

Lappet (Fig. 32 and see instructions on page 57)

Ladies in front of dolls' house (Patterns fig. 79 and see instructions on pages 60, 61 and 73)

Parasols (Figs. 33 and 52 and see instructions on pages 60, 61 and 73)

Parasol

37 pairs 140 Brok, 1 pair gimp 30 DMC

Method

Work in point ground. Begin at **A** and work the shell edge as before (see Figs. 18-20). Add pairs as indicated and follow the diagram. Work Torchon or point ground with rose ground in the top triangles. Join the circle as neatly as possible with sewings; great care is needed when sewing fine threads.

To make up the parasol, cut out the part circle in fabric with bonded lining and form into the parasol shape by sticking the edges together. Cover a cocktail stick with ribbon and push it through the circle. Attach the lace and add a ribbon bow to the top.

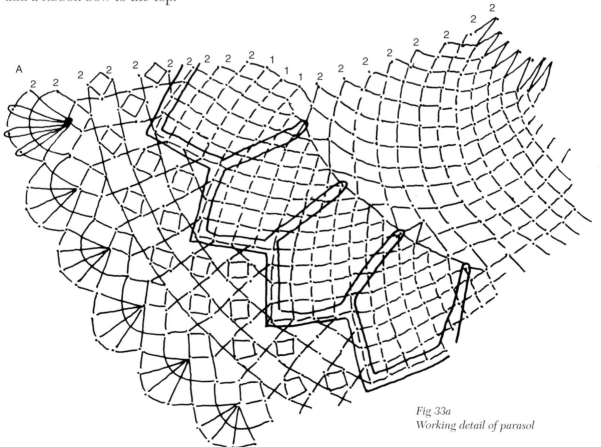

Fig 33a
Working detail of parasol

Fan

**24 pairs 140 Brok, 1 pair gimp
30 DMC**

Method

Set up as indicated and work the
shell edge. Point ground or
Torchon can be used with
honeycomb in the wings. Cross the
gimp at the end of the first wing for
the body and make gimp fingers for
the antennae. Sticks can be made
by cutting the shapes out in
photographic paper and joining
with an earring stud.

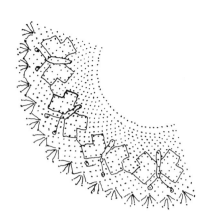

*Fig 34
Fan pricking*

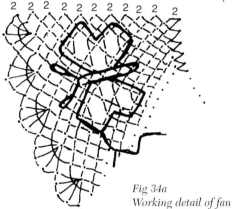

*Fig 34a
Working detail of fan*

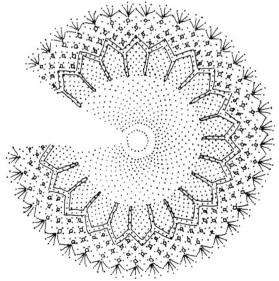

*Fig 33
Parasol pricking*

Torchon Shawl 1

41 pairs 80 Brok, 3 pairs gimp 30 DMC

Method

Start at **A** and make honeycomb rings with
picots on the outside edge. Add pairs inside
the edge trail **A** to **B**. Work the ground with
gimped ovals and blocks of tallies or rose
ground. Turn at **BC** and work the next
triangle. Work all the pairs out into the trail at
the finish, tie off and darn away. If four
triangles are worked, eliminating the trail, the
square will make a tablecloth.

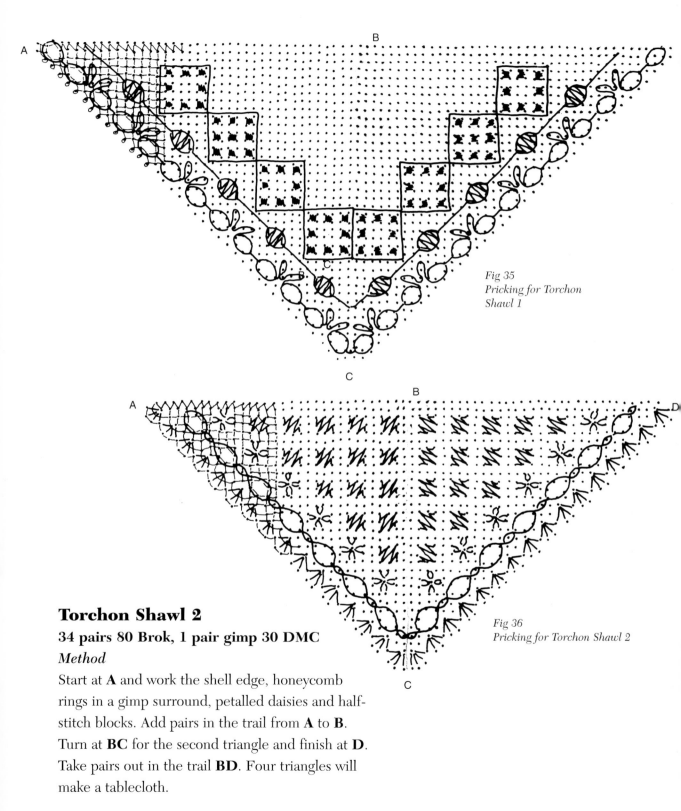

Fig 35
Pricking for Torchon
Shawl 1

Fig 36
Pricking for Torchon Shawl 2

Torchon Shawl 2

34 pairs 80 Brok, 1 pair gimp 30 DMC

Method

Start at **A** and work the shell edge, honeycomb rings in a gimp surround, petalled daisies and half-stitch blocks. Add pairs in the trail from **A** to **B**. Turn at **BC** for the second triangle and finish at **D**. Take pairs out in the trail **BD**. Four triangles will make a tablecloth.

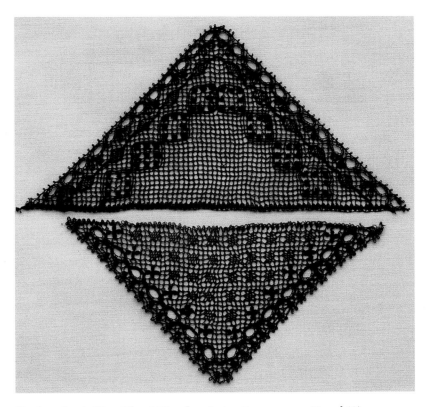

Torchon shawls (Figs. 35 and 36 and see instructions on pages 61 and 62)

Point ground shawl (Fig 37 and see instructions on page 64)

Point Ground Shawl

42 pairs fine silk equivalent to 80 Brok, approx 6 pairs gimp 30 DMC

Method

Start at **A** with a trail at the inner edge and honeycomb rings with gimp fingers on the outer edge. Add pairs as false picots where indicated. Follow the diagram and work point ground and honeycomb stitch. Pairs will accumulate from **B** to **C**. Remove them and bunch the few remaining at C and darn away.

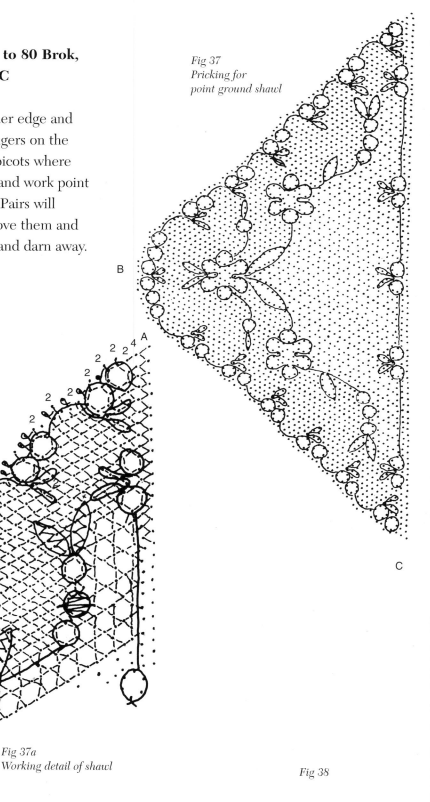

Fig 37
Pricking for point ground shawl

Fig 37a
Working detail of shawl

Fig 38

Parlourmaid

Apron

21 pairs 80 Brok, 2 pairs gimp 30 DMC
Method

Start at **A** and add pairs where indicated.
Follow the diagram, working honeycomb with
mayflowers and a picot edge. Leave pairs at **B**
to work the ringed edge for the apron. Make
an apron front out of fine lawn 7.5 x 6 cm (3 x
2½ in). Make sufficient length to go round the
apron to join at **C**.

Cap

**14 pairs 80 Brok, 1 pair gimp 30 DMC, 1
single gimp**
Method

Work a cloth stitch tape with five pairs from **A**
to **B**. At **B**, add for the honeycomb edge with
picots. Insert the single gimp at B to act as a
gathering thread at the end. Take out pairs at
C as they accumulate and make another cloth
stitch tape to **D**. Darn the threads back and
pull up the single gimp to form the cap.

Frills

**14 pairs 80 Brok, 1 pair gimp 30 DMC, 1
single gimp**
Method

Work as for the cap, leaving out the cloth stitch
tape. Gather the single gimp to fit the shoulder
from bib edge to back apron. Make two.

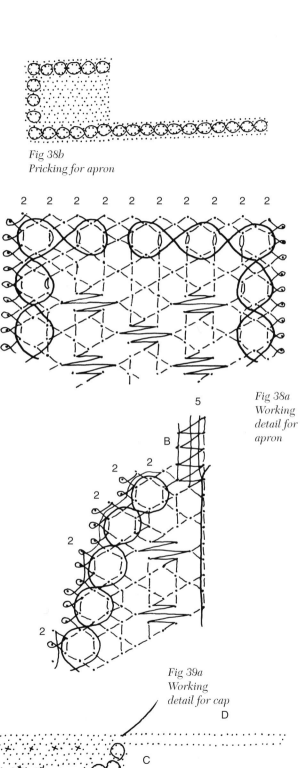

Fig 38b
Pricking for apron

Fig 38a
Working
detail for
apron

Fig 39a
Working
detail for cap

Fig 39b
Pricking
for cap

Edgings for parlourmaid's dress (Figs 38, 39 and see instructions on page 65)

Carrickmacross

Miniature Dress

Method

Trace the pattern to make six repeats and follow the
basic Carrickmacross instructions (see page 21).
Work the bottom edge with loops as in Fig. 39a.

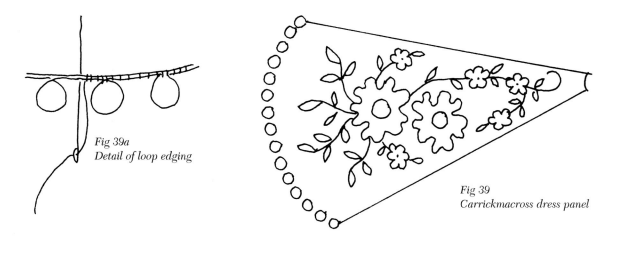

Fig 39a
Detail of loop edging

Fig 39
Carrickmacross dress panel

The lounge with parlourmaid, featuring child with collar and dress edge and cushions
(Figs 26, 21, 26 and 59 and instructions on pages 52, 65 and 84)

The bedroom, with dolls dressing for dinner, featuring Carrickmacross dress, Bertha collar, and black Bertha collar
(Figs. 39, 29 and 28b and see instructions on pages 66 and 53)

Baby

Dress skirt

61 pairs fine silk equivalent to 140 Brok, 3 pairs gimp 30 DMC

Method

This has a bobbin lace skirt with a needlelace bodice. It is worked as half a square, starting at **AB**, turning at **BC**, working **C** to **D** and turning at **B**, with pairs finishing **B** to **E**. Set up two pairs on each pin from **A** to **B** and work the edge as in Fig. 40a and inner flowers as in Fig. 40c. Work in point ground throughout. Tie off the pairs from **B** to **E**; these will be absorbed into the bodice. Gather the top edge to fit the bodice. Alternatively, make the edge as in Fig. 40b and attach to a silk or tulle skirt. The complete square will make a wedding veil.

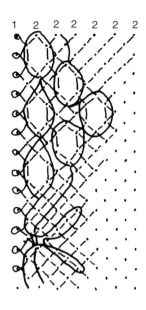

Fig 40a
Working detail of dress edge

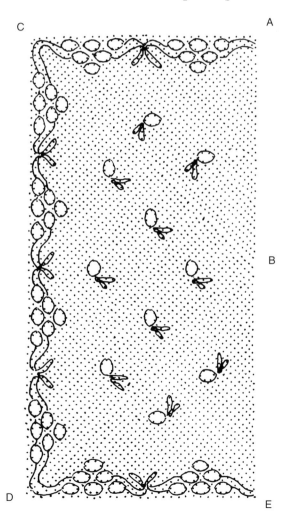

Fig 40
Pricking for baby dress skirt

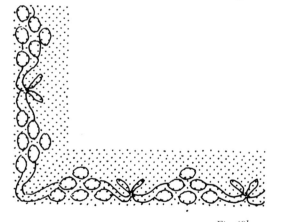

Fig 40b
*Working detail o,
dress edge*

Fig 40c
Working detail of dress skirt

Needlelace

For ¹/₁₂ scale, needlelace is an ideal technique. By using fine threads one can achieve a very tiny edge and it is possible to make entire dresses for babies and children. The simplest form of edge is Point de Venise. It makes a very small shell which can be worked directly into the fabric of the dress or furnishing.

Point de Venise Edging

Method

Attach thread to the edge and make a loop stitch into the edge to the right. Work three loop stitches into this loop and repeat the process. Five loop stitches into the first loop makes a larger shell.

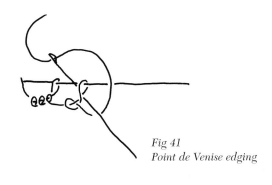

Fig 41
Point de Venise edging

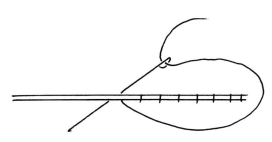

Fig 42
Basic steps - couching

Basic Steps

The stitch used is usually referred to as buttonhole. However, this is not the same as the buttonhole used in embroidery; it resembles blanket or loop stitch.

Method

1. Trace the shape on to firm tracing paper.

2. Cover with plastic film.

3. Tack firmly to a double piece of fabric (sheeting).

4. Couch a double thread with a finer thread (one that will break easily) round the shape, through the paper and the fabric. They should be about 2 mm apart. Secure the couching thread at the back with a few stitches. Start a new thread with a knot as these are taken out at the end. This forms the framework on which the lace is worked.

5. Work filling stitches in the open areas. These are attached to the couched thread and do not go through the fabric.

6. Work bars if indicated.

7. Lay two threads along the same line as the original couching and buttonhole stitch closely over them.

8. Remove the tacking and pull the two pieces of fabric apart, cutting the threads if necessary. If a very fine thread has been used for the couching, these threads will break easily.

9. Remove the lace from the paper and pick out the remaining couching threads.

Worked Bars

Method

Take the thread across the space three times
and loop stitch over the threads.

Couronnes

These are used frequently as decoration and
can be made using a fine knitting needle.

Method

Thread a needle with a long length of thread
and wrap the end several times round the
knitting needle. Make a single buttonhole
stitch round the threads, then gently take the
ring off the knitting needle. Buttonhole
completely round the ring and leave the
thread for sewing into the desired place.

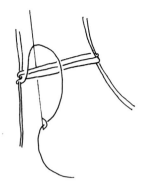

Fig 43
Worked Bars

Brussels Stitch

Method

Introduce a thread by whipping a few stitches
to the outline. With the needle away from you,
work an even row of buttonhole stitches
through the couched threads so that the
stitches lie on the surface. At the end of the
row, take the thread under and over the
couched threads and turn the work.

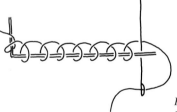

Fig 44
Brussels Stitch – Step 1

Work the next row of stitches from left to
right with the needle towards you, into each
loop of the previous row. Continue until the
space is filled, then whip the filling to the
upper couched threads. Always make sure you
have enough thread to finish the row. Finish
off a thread by whipping it to the couched
thread and start a new one in the same way.

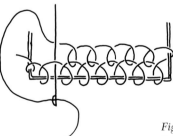

Fig 44a
Brussels Stitch – Step 2

Corded Brussels Stitch

Method

Introduce the thread by whipping
a few stitches to the outline and work a row of
buttonhole stitch. When you reach the right-hand
side, take the thread under and over the
edge and bring it straight back to the left-hand
side. Take it under and over the edge and
repeat row one, including the laid thread.

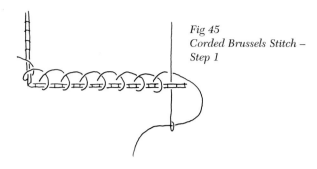

Fig 45
Corded Brussels Stitch –
Step 1

A Row of Holes

This can be used to break up the solid corded
stitch and is worked at regular intervals.

After two or three rows of corded Brussels,
instead of taking the thread across, turn the work
and, with the needle towards you, work a row of
Brussels stitch in alternate stitches. On the return
row work two Brussels stitches in every large loop,
then carry on corded Brussels for another three
rows. This will give an attractive striped effect.

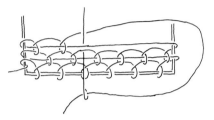

Fig 45a
Corded Brussels Stitch –
Step 2

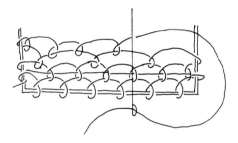

Fig 46
Working a row of holes

Pea Stitch

Work the first row of Brussels stitch from left to
right with the needle away from you. Turn, and
with the needle towards you, work two stitches
and miss two stitches. Turn and work three
stitches in the large loop and one stitch in the
small loop. Repeat the second row, making sure
that the two worked stitches come in the centre of
the previous large loop and the missed stitches are
over the small loop. The following patterns are all
made in needlelace. Follow the Basic Steps 1 to 4
(see page 69).

Use 50 DMC or Guttermans silk 100/3 or as
fine a thread as you can work.

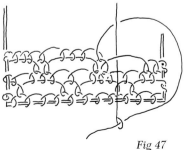

Fig 47
Pea stitch

Baby's Dress in Needlelace

Method (Bodice)

Start the filling at AB. Work corded Brussels, finishing at centre back. After the final buttonholed edge, work a row of Point de Venise round the edge including the neckline. Make a petticoat skirt and attach to the doll's waist. Gather the lace skirt and attach with the edges to the centre front. Fit the bodice on to the baby, over the skirt, and sew into place.

Method (Bonnet)
Back

Work Brussels stitch round the bonnet inner as a continuous circle. When the centre circle is reached, work a woven spider as in Fig. 48a. After the final buttonholed edge, work a row of Point de Venise completely round the back.

Edge

Work corded Brussels from A to B, making holes as in Fig. 47 on the dotted lines. After the final buttonholed edge, work a row of Point de Venise on three sides, A, B and C. Sew the edge to the back so that the Point de Venise protrudes.

Toddler's Dress in Needlelace

Method (Bodice)

Work corded Brussels starting at **AB**, making holes as in Fig. 49 on the dotted lines. After the final buttonholed edge, work a row of Point de Venise completely round the bodice including the neckline.

Method (Skirt)

Start at **AB** and work corded Brussels with two rows of pea stitch at regular intervals, marked by the dotted lines. After the final buttonholed edge, work a row of Point de Venise from **B** to **C**. Instead of Point de Venise, the fan edge from Fig. 18 could be used. Gather the skirt to fit the bodice at the waist and seam the centre back. Fit on to the doll and sew into place.

Method (Bonnet)

Work the bonnet back as for the baby's bonnet. Work pea stitch in the bonnet edge starting at **AB**. After the final buttonholed edge, work a row of Point de Venise on three sides. Attach to the bonnet's back.

Fig 48
Baby dress bodice and bonnet

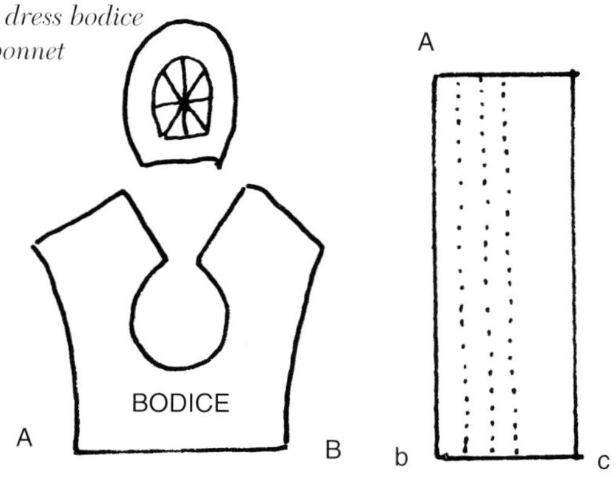

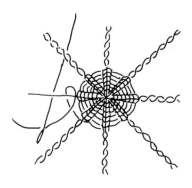

Fig 48a
Working detail of bonnet back

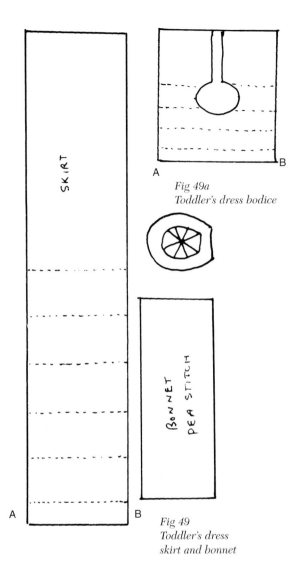

Fig 49a
Toddler's dress bodice

Fig 49
Toddler's dress
skirt and bonnet

Accessories in Needlelace

Method (Round Collar and Cuffs)

Start at **AB** and work in corded Brussels with holes at the intervals marked by the dotted lines. After the final buttonholed edge, work Point de Venise round the outer edge. Work half the collar to make a cuff.

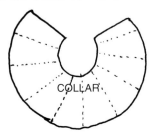

Fig 50
Needlelace collar

Method (Boudoir Cap)

Using Fig 51, start at **AB** and work corded Brussels with holes at intervals marked with dotted lines. After the final buttonholed edge work Point de Venise on edges **ABDC**. Cut a 4 cm (1½ in) diameter circle of net and gather to fit **AC**.

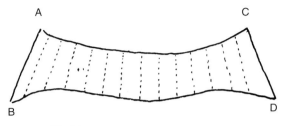

Fig 51
Boudoir cap

Method (Table Centre)

Using Fig. 52 work corded Brussels in each oval and pea stitch in the centre. Make couronnes with Point de Venise edging and sew into the centre of each oval. Work Point de Venise round the outer edge after the final buttonholing.

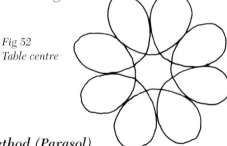

Fig 52
Table centre

Method (Parasol)

A Parasol can be made in the same shape as the table centre (see page 81) using seven ovals. Fill each oval with pea stitch, with corded Brussels in the centre. After the final buttonholing, work Point de Venise on the outer edge. Instead of Point de Venise, any bobbin lace edge from Figs. 18–20 can be used.

Boudoir cap with edge
(see Figs. 51 and 18 and instructions on page 73)

Toddler in needlelace dress with edge
(see Figs. 49 and 18 and instructions on pages 72 and 73)

Baby doll in dress with needlelace bonnet
(see Figs. 40, 48 and 49 and instructions on pages 68, 72 and 73)

Table centre and mat
(see Figs. 52 and 55 and instructions on pages 73 and 80)

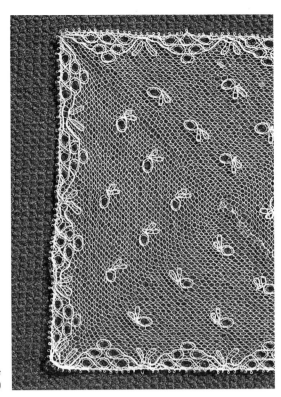

Skirt of baby's dress
(see Fig. 40 and instructions on page 68)

Doll at table, showing tablecloth in needlelace, children in dresses and boy's collar
(see Figs. 53, 49 and 50 and instructions on pages 72 and 77)

CHAPTER THREE
DOLLS' HOUSES

Dolls' houses have been in existence for about three hundred years, though the most prolific period was in the eighteenth and nineteenth centuries. They were usually referred to as baby houses and many furnished ones can be seen in museums and country houses. They are examples of the prevailing domestic architecture and furnishings, frozen in time, and they nearly always have their small occupants in residence.

The earliest surviving example is probably the Nuremburg kitchen of the mid-eighteenth century. It consisted of a box with three walls and a floor about 45 x 30 cm (18 x 12 in), fully kitted out with all kinds of kitchenware: utensils, pans, tea services, stoves, dressers, tables and chairs. Single rooms seem to have been very popular and were made in Germany and the Low Countries from the early seventeenth century. They were often designed as shops and were practical as they could be easily set up and packed away at the end of the day. Boxes such as these are a good way to start a dolls' house project before committing yourself to a large dolls' house.

The large dolls' house seems to have started life in Holland in the seventeenth century, where rich merchants loved to have reproductions of their own houses and furnishings. No expense was spared and the finest furniture makers, silversmiths, and artists were commissioned to create these miniature houses. They were certainly not intended for children. The result was housed in a glass cabinet which was locked and only later did this develop into a fronted dolls' house with suitable brickwork, doors and windows. By the twentieth century it became a child's toy and this is when dolls' houses were commercially produced.

Today there are many choices of house both ready-made and in kit form. It is also possible to build your own and there are many books for guidance. Furniture is available, some of which can be furbished with Petit Point or Florentine Embroidery worked on fine silk canvas or fine linen. Carpets can be made in cross stitch on counted thread material and can be worked in stranded cotton or fine wool. The room settings in the photographs throughout this book show some of the possibilities.

The Dining Room

Tablecloth in Needlelace

This is a miniature copy of a tape lace (Battenburg) cloth. The tape outline consists of a buttonholed edge with simplified fillings. Four repeats make a small cloth suitable fora round table. The pattern shown fits a dining table or it will make a bedspread.

Method

Use 30 DMC and couch a double thread round the design. Work Brussels stitch in the corner flowers. Take a single thread to criss-cross the narrow leaf shapes and make worked bars to hold the shapes together. Lay two threads round the design and buttonhole closely. Buttonhole the edge on to a piece of fine lawn.

Fig 53
Needlelace cloth

Needlelace tablecloth (see Fig. 53 and instructions on page 77)

Hexagon tablecloth in bobbin lace
(see Fig. 54 and instructions on pages 80 and 82)

The dining room set for tea, showing tablecloth, chair seats in Florentine embroidery, and carpet in cross stitch (see Fig. 54 and instructions on pages 80-81)

Dining room with tablecloth made from quilt pattern (see Fig. 63 and instructions on pages 88 and 89)

Hexagon Tablecloth

Method (Inset)

**20 pairs fine silk equivalent to
100 Brok. 2 pairs gimp 30 DMC**

Work in point ground. Set with three pairs at
A and add one pair on each of the others on
the diagonal. Add one pair of gimp at **B** and
one pair at **C**. Follow the diagram for working
and turn at each section. Join at **A**.

Method (Edge)

19 pairs, one single and 1 pair gimp

Set up with three pairs at **A** and one on each
pin to **B**. Add a single gimp at **A** and work
picot edge as shown. Work flowers and
honeycomb blocks following the diagram.
Turn after each section and join as neatly as
possible. Attach to a piece of silk or very fine
lawn with four-sided stitch and cut away
behind the inset. Silk drapes better than
cotton over the table edge.

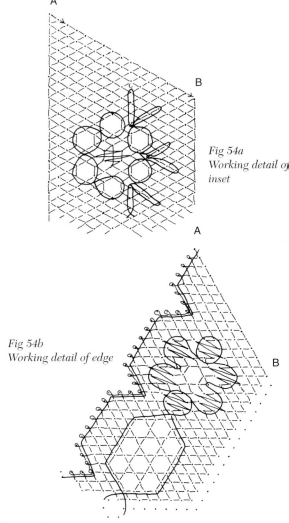

Fig 54a
Working detail of
inset

Fig 54b
Working detail of edge

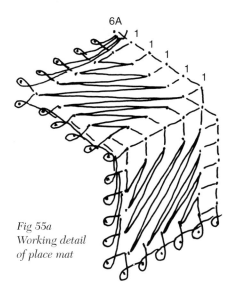

Fig 55a
Working detail
of place mat

Place Mat

11 pairs 80 Brok

Method

Follow the diagram, starting at **A** with six pairs
and working section by section. Join as neatly
as possible.

Fig 55
Pricking for place mat

Table Centre

20 pairs 100 Brok, 1 pair gimp 30 DMC

Method

Work in point ground. Set up two pairs at **A** and **B** and one pair on each pin on the diagonal. Follow the diagram and work section by section. Work the shells as for the edge in Fig 20. Join as neatly as possible.

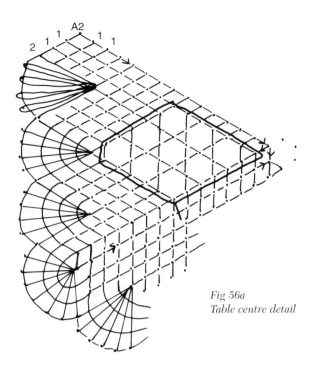

Fig 56a
Table centre detail

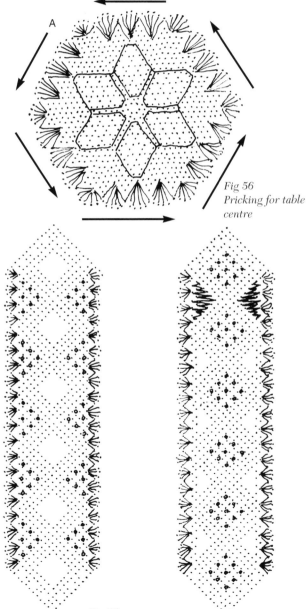

Fig 56
Pricking for table centre

Table or Sideboard runner

25 pairs 120 Brok

Method

Work in Torchon. Set up as shown and follow the diagram. The cloth or half-stitch blocks and rose ground can be interchanged as shown in the two prickings. Finish by taking pairs out as they accumulate and tying the remainder in a bunch. Darn the threads away.

Fig 57a
Working detail of table runner

Fig 57
Prickings for table runners

Fig 54
Hexagon tablecloth edge and inset prickings

Chair backs and cushions (see Figs. 58 and 59 and instructions on page 84)

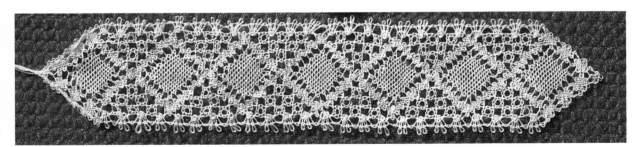

Table runner (see Fig. 57 and instructions on page 81)

The Lounge

Torchon Chair Backs

23 pairs 50 DMC, 2 pairs gimp 30 DMC
Method

Follow the diagrams, setting up pairs as
indicated. Carry the pairs along at the end so
that they finish in a bunch. Tie these to form
a tassel.

Torchon Cushions

14 pairs 80 Brok, 1 pair gimp 30 DMC
Method

Four different cushions worked as Torchon
squares with a honeycomb ringed edge, rose
ground, cloth stitch blocks, spiders or hearts.
Follow the diagram and work each section
as shown.

Start at **A** with two pairs and one pair
on each pin to **B**. Join neatly and sew to
a backing.

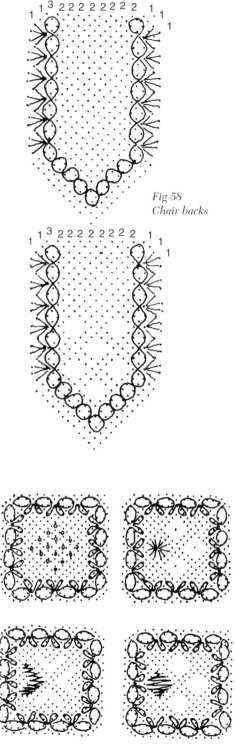

Fig 58
Chair backs

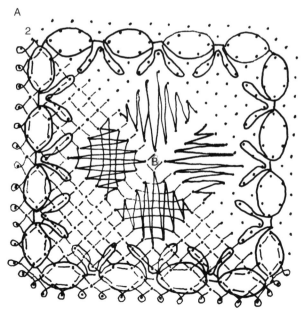

Fig 59a
Working diagram of cushion

Fig 59
Cushions and squares for quilt

The Bedroom

Dressing Table cover

60 pairs 120 Brok, 1 pair gimp 30 DMC

This is an extension of the edge in Fig. 23 with slight variations.

Method

Start with two pairs on each pin from **A** to **B** and work as shown. Work a shell edge, cloth stitch blocks, honeycomb rings and honeycomb ground. Make a 20 cm (8 in) length and a 23 cm (9 in) length of the edge shown in Fig. 23. Attach the narrow one, slightly gathered, to the deep one and fit round the dressing table.

Bed Linen

Method

Make sheets in fine lawn with edges and insets from Fig. 20. Make pillowcases to match. If the lawn is even weave, the insets can be worked in drawn thread.

Lace Patchwork Quilt 1

Method

Make squares of lace from the cushion pattern (see Fig. 59) and join alternately with squares of fine lawn with embroidered butterflies in shadow work (see Fig. 61). Use the edge pattern shown in Fig. 25 for the surround.

Fig 60
Pricking for dressing table edge

Fig 61
Pattern for embroidery

Fig 62
Pricking for Torchon Quilt 1

Sheets and pillowcases with edges (see Figs. 18 and 20 and instructions on page 85)

Doll at dressing table showing edges, boudoir cap and petticoat edge
(see Figs. 23, 60, 51 and 24 and instructions on pages 48, 49 and 85)

Torchon Quilt 1

32 pairs 50 DMC, 1 pair gimp perlé 12
Method
Using Fig. 62 begin at **A** with two pairs and add one pair on each pin from **A** to **B**. Work the triangle **ABC** with cloth stitch trails and rose ground blocks. Make a picot honeycomb ringed edge as for the cushions (see Fig. 59). Turn at **C** and work **CBDE**. Turn and work triangle **DEF**. Turn and work **FDBA**. Make sewings from **D** to **B**. Sew out and join at AB.

Torchon Quilt 2

36 pairs Tannen 50 white or cream, 2 pairs gimp perlé 12
or 33 pairs Tannen 50 white, 3 pairs coloured, 2 pairs gimp perlé 12
Method
Using Fig. 63 start with three pairs at **A** and one pair on each pin to **B**. If using colour add a coloured pair instead of a white at the start of each trail marked **X**. These carry on through. Work the triangle **ABC**, turn and work **CBDE**.

Work the centre with half a rose ground as shown in Fig. 63a. Turn at **E** and work triangle **EDF**, turn and work **FDBA**, making sewings in the central rose ground. Join finally at **AB**.

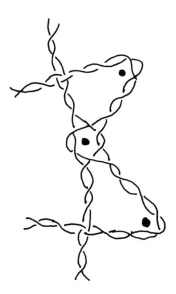

Fig 63a
Working detail
of Quilt 2

Fig 63
Pricking for Torchon Quilt 2

Patchwork lace quilt with butterflies (Fig. 61), cushion (Fig. 59) and edge (Fig. 25) and see instructions on pages 84 and 85

Torchon quilt (Fig. 63 and see instructions on pages 88 and 89)

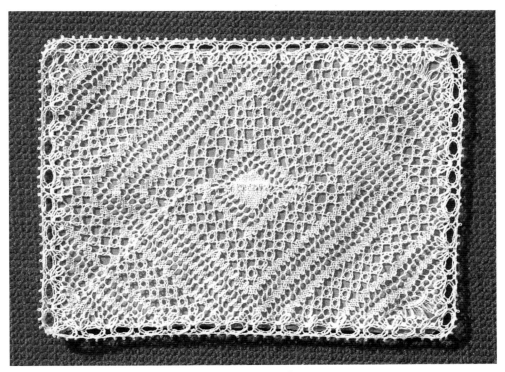

Torchon quilt (Fig. 62 and see instructions on pages 86 and 87)

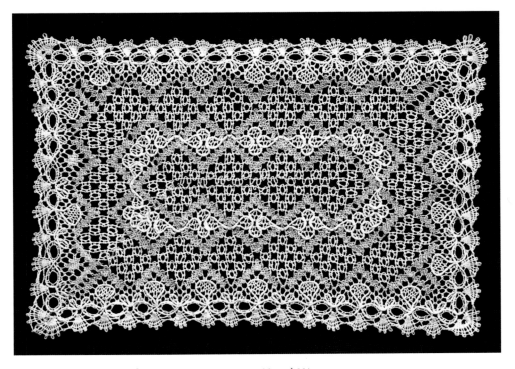

Torchon quilt (Fig. 63 and see instructions on pages 88 and 89)

Cot Quilt

26 pairs 100 Brok

Method

Set up two pairs on each pin from **A** to **B**, and work rose ground and cloth stitch diamonds. Tie off the threads at the end and cut off. The edge will cover these. Make a 7.5 cm (3 in) length of Spanish fan (see Fig. 18). Sew the lace to a 32 x 38 mm (1¼ x 1½ in) rectangle of lawn made into a small bag and attach the edge round it, gathering slightly at the corners.

Note: In order to house the quilt, you could make a cot from firm card, with measurements as shown in Fig. 65, patterns **A** and **B**. Cut **C** in slightly thinner card so that it will curve easily. Cover all the pieces with material and assemble. Bend **A** on the dotted lines and join **A** to **A** by sewing. Sew in base **B** and attach **C** to the cot edge and the curved back.

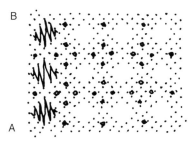

Fig 64
Cot quilt pricking

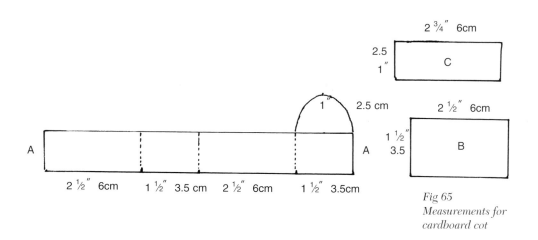

Fig 65
Measurements for cardboard cot

Cot Edge

31 pairs 100 Brok, 2 pairs gimp 30 DMC

Method

Start at **A** and set up pairs to **B**. Follow the diagram, working blocks of rose ground with cloth stitch hearts. Cross pairs at **C** to form holes for threading ribbon. Work four repeats, each 23 cm (9¼ in) long, and join into a circle.

Curved Edge

26 pairs 100 Brok, 2 pairs gimp 30 DMC

Method

Work the edge in the same way as for the cot edge, but there are no ribbon holes. Work the pattern length. Attach this edge to the head piece, sewing it into place. Thread narrow ribbon through the edge and gather to fit, then attach this round the cot. Sew at intervals to keep it in place. Make a small mattress from lawn, padded with cotton wool, and make a small pillow. Edge the pillow in Point de Venise or edge with Spanish fan as in Fig 18.

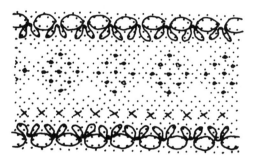

Fig 66a
Pricking for cot edge

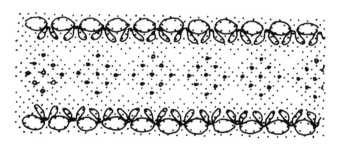

Fig 66c
Pricking for curved edge

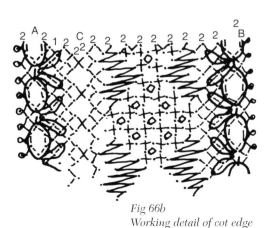

Fig 66b
Working detail of cot edge

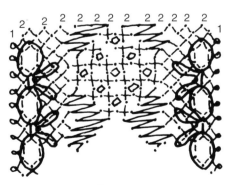

Fig 66d
Working detail of cot curved edge

Cot quilt and cot edge (see Figs. 64 and 66 and instructions pages 92-93)

Cot made up (see Figs. 65 and 66 and instructions on pages 92-93)

Curtains with bobbin lace strips (Fig. 67 and instructions on page 96)

Net embroidered curtain (Fig. 68) and curtain made from quilt (Fig. 62) cut in half (see instructions on pages 97 and 88)

Curtains

Method (Bobbin Lace strips)

18 pairs 100 Brok, 1 pair gimp

30 DMC

Set up two pairs on each pin from **A** to **B** and work Torchon or point ground with butterflies as shown. Start each one at the body end and cut off at each antennae. Work a strip to window-length and tie off the ends. These will be at the top of the window. Several strips can be sewn together to make a complete curtain, or they can be sewn at intervals with net.

You can also make complete curtains by using the dressing table pattern in two pieces, shell edges meeting, or make a café type curtain to cover half the window only. Torchon Quilt 1 may also be used, and can be cut into two pieces. Bind the cut edges with the chosen curtain material. It is easier to work the whole quilt and cut it than to work two separate pieces.

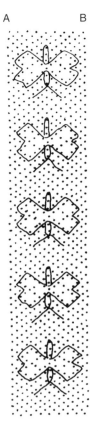

Fig 67
Pricking for Butterfly strip for curtains

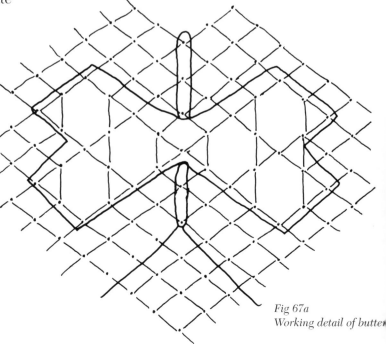

Fig 67a
Working detail of butter

Method (Net Embroidery Curtains)

Use stranded cotton for the net embroidery curtains; two strands for the outline and one strand for the filling. This is the quickest way to make lace curtains, the patterning formed by darning on net. There are numerous stitch formations and straight, curved and pointed edges are possible. The pattern shown has been used for both shop and lounge curtains but once the principle is understood, more heavily patterned curtains can be achieved.

Net is available in many sizes. Always set it into an embroidery frame, and stretch tightly. Follow the diagram and work the diamond outline first with two strands. Work the daisy filling with one strand; each daisy follows on to the next one. Buttonhole the edges of the diamonds and cut away the net.

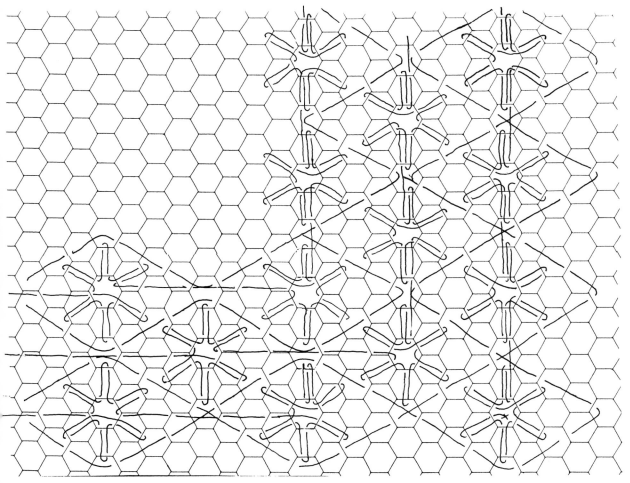

Fig 68
Working detail of net embroidery for curtains

CHAPTER FOUR
DRESSING DOLLS

Dolls can be purchased in kit form with a porcelain head and limbs and patterns for a cloth body. The heads can be bought with a shoulder or with just a neck, and it is important to note this before deciding on the dress style. Arms can be elbow-length or above and legs can be to the knee or above. Wigs can be purchased separately to style for the intended period.

The patterns in this chapter are as authentic in cut as is possible, given that one is working in quarter-scale.

There follows some useful points to remember when dressing dolls:
• Make the doll's body soft round the waist so that it can be corseted.
• Always make a corset as this gives the required shape to the figure when dressed.
• Wire the arms so that the doll can be posed with a fan or parasol. Take the wire from one arm to the other, making a loop in the body to stop it moving.
• Sew through the knee-line and hip-line if you want the doll to be seated. The doll will then bend well at these joints.

• Use tubular finger bandage for stockings, small-patterned material for dresses, and fine lawn for underwear.
• Remember that prior to 1860 the sewing machine had not been invented, so dresses should be hand sewn for maximum authenticity.

The following standard articles of clothing are useful for most period clothing outfits. In addition to these you can also make useful trimmings with long lengths of crossway, folding the edges to the middle and running a gathering thread through the centre, catching in the folded edges. This makes an attractive ruching which has been used on the Late Regency doll's costume and on the Victorian bonnet. Pleated frills make a good decoration at the hemline, but pink the edges before pleating. Small round beads with worked loops make good front fastenings. Use small hooks and worked bars for a back opening.

Make petticoats, chemises and pantaloons with drawstrings; this eliminates the need for openings and makes the material easier to gather. The gathers can then be placed where fullness is required. For patterns see pages 104-123.

Standard Period Clothing

Corset

A satisfactory corset can be made in stiff Vilene.

Method

Using Fig. 69 make darts where indicated and sew Rigilene (available from most haberdashers') in strips over each dart and either side of the centre back. Fold the back edge over the Rigilene and thread fine ribbon or cord through at intervals to lace the doll tight. If the ribbon or cord is threaded through a large needle, it can be pulled through without having to make holes. Place on the doll first and lace into position; no turnings are needed. Alternatively, use stiff, iron-on Vilene with a fancy material and trim the corset with lace. Add a 1 cm (¼ in) turning to the pattern, and make small hems at the top and bottom.

Chemise

This is worn under the corset. Back and front are the same; the length of body and sleeve should be adjusted before cutting out.

Method

Using Fig. 10, join the shoulders with small French seams and make a small rolled hem at the neckline and sleeve edges. Attach lace to these and run a gathering thread on the dotted line to pull up the sleeve and neck to fit the doll. This will allow for a high or low neckline. Make a 1 cm (¼ in) hem at the bottom using any narrow lace edge from Chapter 2.

Corset and pantaloons (Figs. 69 and 71 and instructions on page 99)

Pantaloons

These are made as two separate legs with a split round the crutch.

Method

Using Fig. 71, cut each out in lawn, either full length, or cut off at the dotted line and add a frill. Add lace to the bottom and insets and give each leg a small hem from waist to crutch. Make a 1cm (¼ in) hem at the waist and thread a cord through. Pull this up to fit the doll under the corset.

Petticoats

These can be made from straight pieces of material: 68 cm (27 in) by the length from waist to ankle is adequate.

Method

Make a narrow hem at the top and gather with a cord. Add lace or broderie anglaise to the hem. A crinoline is made in the same way, but make three small tucks at regular intervals from hem to waist. Thread narrow cane or wire through these tucks and pull the material to make a graduated cone shape.

Elizabethan Costume

See page 9 for general historical fashion details of the Elizabethan era.

Elizabethan dress

See photograph on page 2 and Figs. 72a-d for the bodice and sleeve patterns.

Method

Choose plain material or self-patterned material in black for the basic dress with a patterned or embroidered fabric for the underskirt. Make a corset with slightly deeper darts and lace on to the doll.

Make the skirt pattern by drawing a circle with the circumference of the doll's waistline. Measure from the circle's edge to the floor for the skirt's length and draw another circle. Cut the circle in half and use half for the underskirt pattern and half for the overskirt. Cut out in paper towel and fit to the doll. When satisfied, cut out in the material and make up, leaving an opening at the back of the underskirt. Make a small hem at the waistline and attach to the doll with a hook and bar fastening.

Iron soft Vilene to the bodice, sew the front dart and join the shoulder seams. Gather the blackwork sleeve and gauze to fit the armhole and sew into place. Sew the side and sleeve seams. Make a small hem at the neckline and at the bottom of the bodice, sewing pearls to the lower edge. Attach hooks and worked bars to the centre back opening and fit on to the doll. Cut the false sleeve out in material and coloured lining and join the two together on the wrong side, leaving the top shoulder edge open. Turn through and press. Oversew AB to AB and attach the false sleeve to the shoulder. Make the padded sleeve roll by folding over and stuffing lightly with cotton wool.

Wrap pearls round the roll and attach to the shoulder. Fold a 15 cm (6 in) x 5 cm (2 in) strip of material lengthwise and sew the edges. Stuff with cotton wool to make a bum roll and tie round the waist under the skirts.

Head-dress

Method

Using Fig. 72e cut two pieces of fabric and one of heavy-duty Vilene. Sew round on the wrong side with the Vilene on top, leaving AB open. Turn through, press and decorate the edge with pearls. Attach to the head. Attach the lace collar and cuffs. If the doll has a good, low neckline, the front neckline can be cut lower.

Georgian Costume

See page 14 for general historical fashion details of the Georgian era.

Lady's Costume

(See photograph on page 19 and Figs. 73a-73c.) Choose a striped, soft material and use iron-on Vilene on the bodice and sleeves.

Method

Make up the quilted petticoat and attach to the doll over a corset with a drawstring. Sew the front dart of the bodice and make a stitched tuck in the back as indicated. Join shoulder seams AB to AB and side seams CD to CD. Make up the sleeve and gather to fit the armhole, sewing into place by matching the notches. Gather or pleat the skirt to fit the bodice and turn a hem on the front edge. Attach hooks and bars to the centre front and make small hems at the neckline, sleeves and lower front bodice. Attach narrow lace around the neck and the two ruffles to the sleeves with the deeper part to the back.

The hat can be made in straw (bought in strips). Coil a strip into a circle and sew it together to form a 5 cm (2 in) diameter. Continue sewing to form a crown 1 cm (¼ in) high and a brim of 5 cm (2 in). Trim with silk or lace roses and narrow lace under the brim.

Man's Costume

(See photograph on page 15 and Fig. 74.) Choose velvet for the suit with a matching lining and brocade for the waistcoat.

Method

To make the flared jacket, join pattern pieces AB to AB and cut out in paper towel, making adjustments where necessary. Make a corset and fit (see page 99). Make breeches by using the pantaloon pattern cut off to the knee. Sew the crutch and make a drawstring round the waist. Make hems at the bottom and fold on the outer edge so that they fit tight. Add gold beads as buttons. Make a shirt from the chemise pattern with sleeves to the wrist. Gather the neckline into a small band to fit the neck, opening at the back. Gather the 23 cm (9 in) length of lace to form a jabot, and attach to the front. Attach the ruffles to the sleeve's edge and gather to fit the wrist.

Make up the waistcoat (Figs. 74a and b), sewing the side and shoulder seams but leaving the front and back open. Make hems on the fronts and backs, at the hemline and

round the armholes. Permanently close the front with an overlap and sew on gold beads as buttons. Place on the doll and lace at the back.

Cut out the sleeve (Fig. 74e) with an extra cuff piece from the dotted line. Sew the cuff round on the wrong side and turn through. Make mock buttonholes where indicated by couching a gold thread round the marked line, turning back the cuff and sewing beads as buttons over the buttonholes. Then sew the sleeve seam. Make two pocket flaps (Fig. 74f), sew and turn through. Make mock buttonholes and attach to the jacket fronts. Sew bead buttons on top of the mock buttonholes.

Cut out the lining to the same size as the jacket and sew shoulder and side seams of both. Attach the lining completely round the hem, fronts and centre back to B. Leave the centre back open from B to the neck. Turn through and press. Make mock buttonholes at centre back and centre front. Attach the sleeves, gathering to fit, and finish off the neckline with the lining. Attach bead buttons to the opposite sides. The jacket will fall into soft pleats at the side.

Use a female wig with straight hair. Take the front hair and make two rolls away from the forehead. Sew into place. Form three rolls on either side of the head and sew again. Place the back hair into a small black bag, gathered with a black ribbon which ties round the neck. Make a black ribbon bow and sew on to the black bag. Black stockings and shoes sometimes come in the doll-making kit.

Regency Costume

See page 20 for general historical fashion details of the Regency era.

Regency Dress 1805

(See page 22.) Choose pale colours in soft material for the underskirt and underbodice.

Method

Using Figs. 75a-c cut the bodice and sleeves in net as well as in your chosen material and make up as one piece of fabric. Attach the lace to the underskirt and gather the top. The bodice comes just below the bust and can be darted or gathered (the dotted line is for the dress neckline and the top one for the Spencer). The shoulder seam lies well to the back. The line AB is normally a seam, but you will find it easier to make a small dart. Join the shoulder seams, and gather the sleeve to fit the armhole. Sew into place and then sew the side and sleeve seams. Gather the skirt to fit the bodice, keeping the gathers to the back. Make small hems at the neckline, sleeve and hemline and add a narrow lace to the neck and sleeve. Fasten the back with hooks and worked bars. Make the petticoat (the same size as the skirt) and a chemise and pantaloons (see page 99).

Spencer 1805

Use a similar shade of material to the dress backed with soft, iron-on Vilene for the Spencer jacket.

Method

Make the bodice as for the dress but with the high neckline. Gather the puff sleeve (see Figs. 75d and e) to fit the armhole and the lower sleeve and sew into place. Sew the side and sleeve seams. Make small hems at the front, neckline, sleeve and bottom. Fasten the jacket with loops and buttons or hooks and worked bars.

Dress 1820

(See page 26 and Fig. 76.) Choose pale colours in silk taffeta or a similar stiff material that will give the skirt its bell shape.

Method

Make a chemise, pantaloons and a petticoat with a frill at the bottom (see page 99). Cut out the bodice in paper towel and adjust to fit well. Use soft, iron-on Vilene on the bodice. Make up the bodice, marking side seam AB and make a small hem at the neck.

The Beret sleeve is formed from a circle with a hole in it for the arm. This should lie to the front so a left and right sleeve must be cut. Work close buttonhole stitches round the hole and cut out. Gather the circle to fit the armhole, and try on the doll at this stage to ensure the fit. The gathers will be very close and must be sewn with firm backstitches into the armhole. Make the cap sleeve by cutting fabric and lining, sewing together on the wrong side and turning through. Trim with ruching.

Gather the lace frill and attach to the sleeve head. Cover with the cap and sew this neatly on top. Cut a skirt 61 cm (24 in) by length to ankle, and sew the back seam leaving a 5 cm (2 in) opening. Make the bottom hem and trim with ruching and lace. Gather to fit the bodice and attach hooks and worked bars to the back opening. The bodice should be off-the-shoulder and the sleeves puffed out.

Victorian Costume

Victorian doll's costume with crinoline

(See page 31.) Choose small-patterned material with a matching plain fabric for the jacket. Use iron-on Vilene on the jacket.

Method

Make a corset. Cover this with the jacket material and edge the top with the lace edging used on the jacket. Make pantaloons with insets, and a crinoline petticoat (see page 99).

Method (Tiered skirt)

Cut three 92 cms (36 in) strips, width 12 cm (4½ in), 15 cm (6 in) and 18 cm (7 in). Bind these with crossway from the jacket. Cut a half-circle pattern as for the Elizabethan skirt and use for the tiered base. Join the seams of circle and strips and gather the strips to fit the circle's base, the first to the waist, the second 6 cm (2½ in and the third 10 cm (4 in) from the waist. Make a waistband and attach to the skirt, fastening with a button and loop. Cut two 8 x 15 cm (2 x 3 in) strips of the dress fabric and gather them for undersleeves to the wrist and upper arm. These could be made in lace, net or broderie anglaise.

Method (Jacket)

Sew the bodice darts front and back, fit and sew the sleeve into the armhole and sew sleeve and side seams. Make hems at the neckline, front edges, bottom and sleeve edges and apply the lace edge. The corset front shows and the jacket fastens at the waist with a hook and worked bar.

Victorian doll's costume with bustle

(See page 38) Use a doll with a low neckline and long arms. With plain silk taffeta or moiré, make a corset, knee-length pantaloons and petticoat.

Method (Skirt)

Using Figs. 78a and b cut two pieces, 28 cm (11 in) by the length from waist to floor and 33 cm (13 ins), waist to floor but 5 cm (2 in) longer at the centre back for the bustle. Cut the apron front and back pieces, and make a small hem for each. Attach folded net, pleated frill or lace to the edges. Pleat the front and pin to the front skirt sides. Gather or pleat the back and pin to the back. Join the skirt seams, leaving a small opening on one side, and gather the skirts into a waistband.

Method (Bodice)

Cut the bodice where indicated (see Figs. 78c and d), sewing the dart and the back seam, and gather or pleat the peplum into it. Sew the side and shoulder seams. Make small hems at the neckline and bodice bottom and attach folded net, pleated frill or lace to the lower edge. Attach lace roses and leaves to the neckline and at skirt sides. Make a large stuffed pad to tie round the waist as a bustle.

Flapper Costume

Flapper Dress (1920)
Method

The lace dress on page 43 has a petticoat cut from the same shape as the bodice plus 5 cm (2 in). Make bloomers from the pantaloon pattern cut off at the knee and gathered. Sew the crutch.

CHAPTER FIVE
THE PATTERNS

Always trace and cut patterns out in soft paper towel or nappy liner first. Pin together and fit on to the doll over the corset, making any necessary adjustments. Patterns can be enlarged or reduced to fit any size doll. If traced they are suitable for 40-46 cm (16-18 in) dolls. There are no turnings allowed so add 1 cm (¼ in) to the patterns.

Use soft, iron-on Vilene on the bodices; this makes them easier to handle, and only single turnings will be necessary for the edges. Always sew the bodice shoulder seams and darts first, then sew in the sleeve heads, and finally sew the side seams of the bodice and the sleeve seams at the same time.

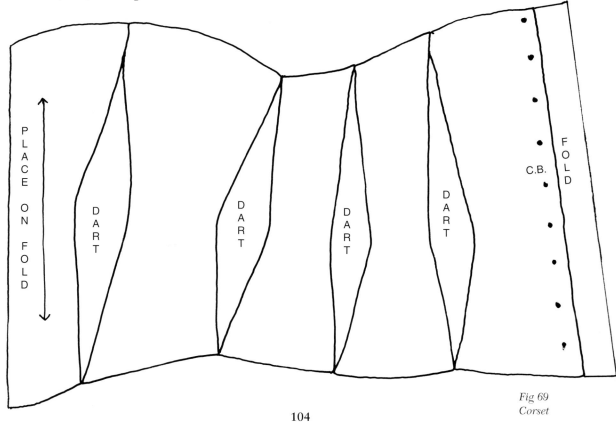

Fig 69
Corset

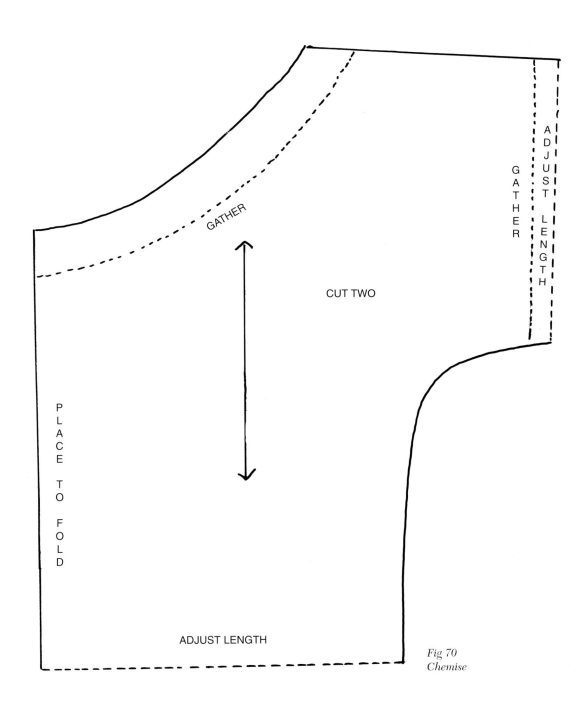

GATHER

ADJUST LENGTH

GATHER

CUT TWO

PLACE TO FOLD

ADJUST LENGTH

Fig 70
Chemise

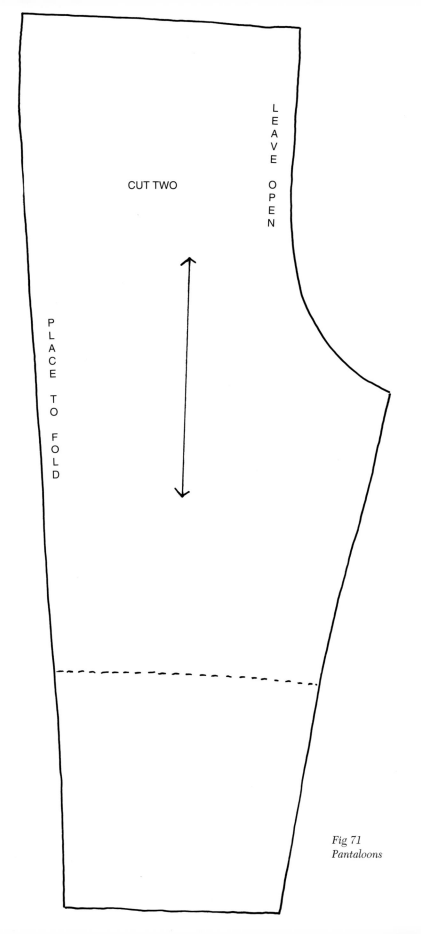

CUT TWO

LEAVE OPEN

PLACE TO FOLD

Fig 71
Pantaloons

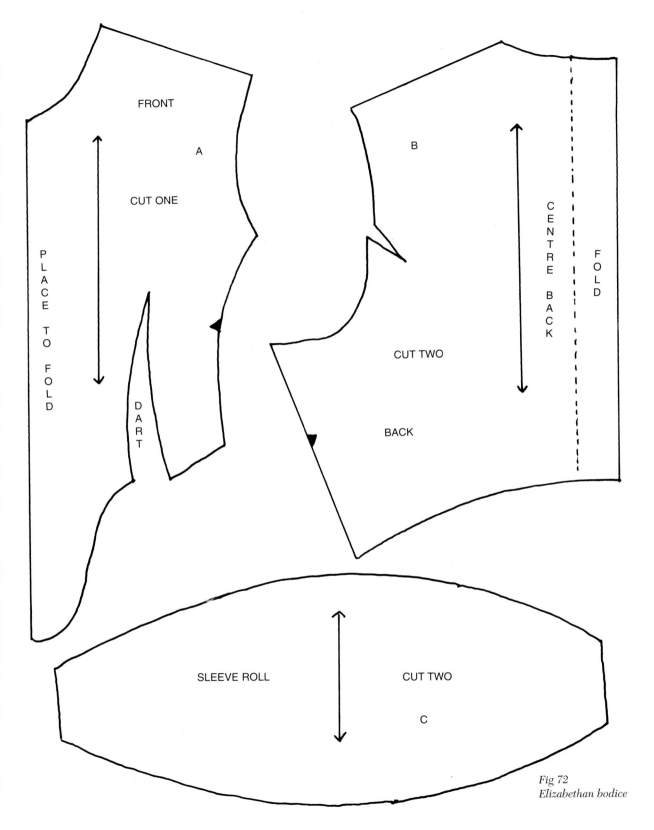

FRONT

A

CUT ONE

PLACE TO FOLD

DART

B

CENTRE BACK

FOLD

CUT TWO

BACK

SLEEVE ROLL   CUT TWO

C

Fig 72
Elizabethan bodice

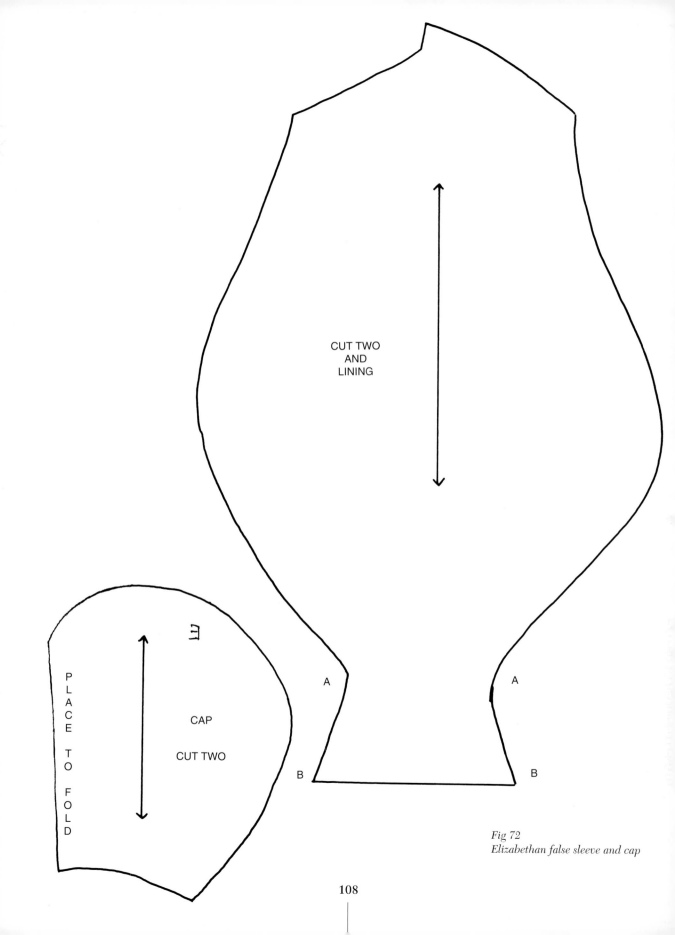

CUT TWO
AND
LINING

PLACE TO FOLD

CAP

CUT TWO

A

B

A

B

Fig 72
Elizabethan false sleeve and cap

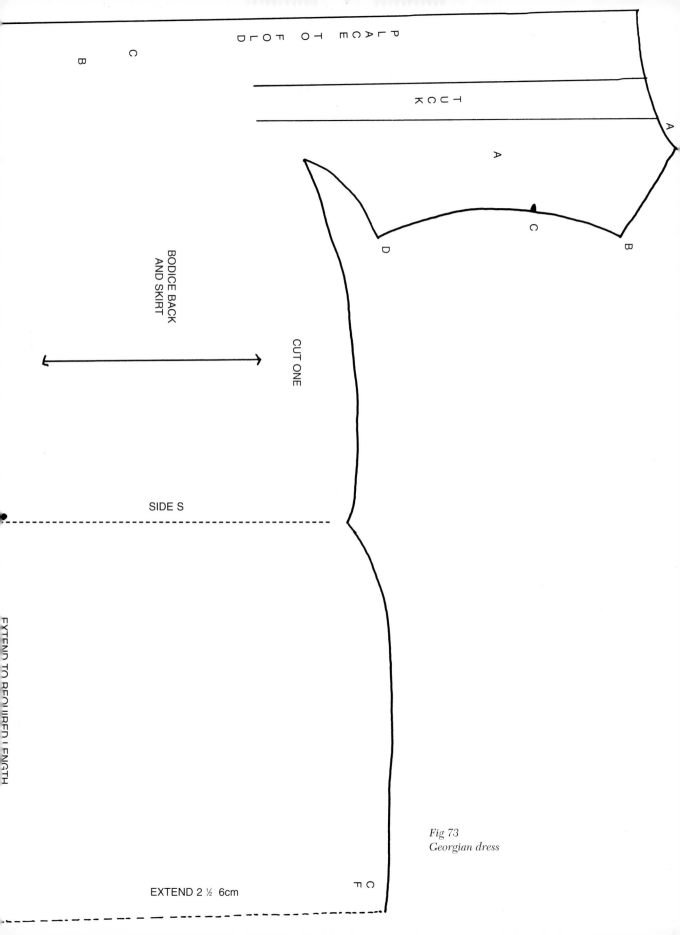

PLACE TO FOLD

WAIST

B C
A

A

C

D B

BODICE BACK
AND SKIRT

CUT ONE

SIDE S

EXTEND TO REQUIRED LENGTH

Fig 73
Georgian dress

EXTEND 2 ½ 6cm

C F

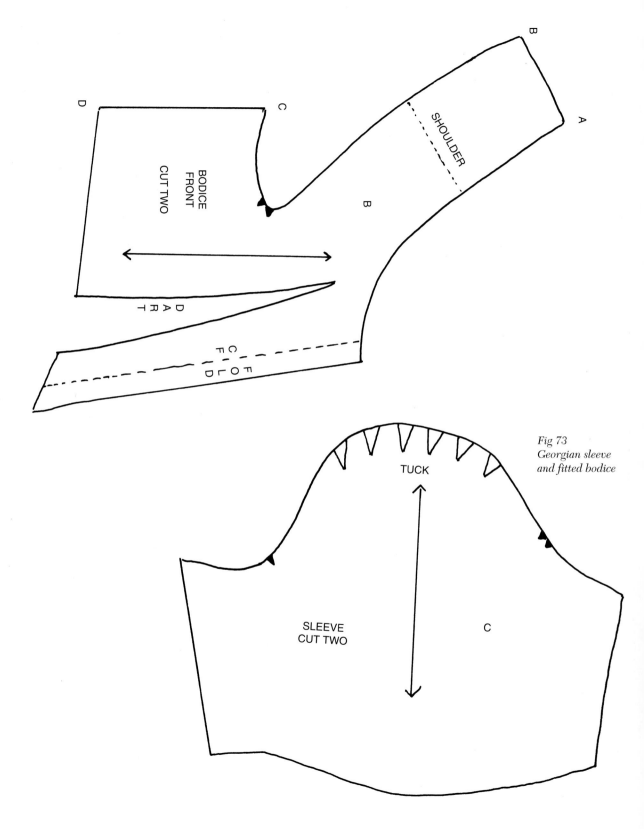

BODICE
FRONT
CUT TWO

SHOULDER

A

B

B

C

D

D R A F T

C F O L D

Fig 73
*Georgian sleeve
and fitted bodice*

TUCK

SLEEVE
CUT TWO

C

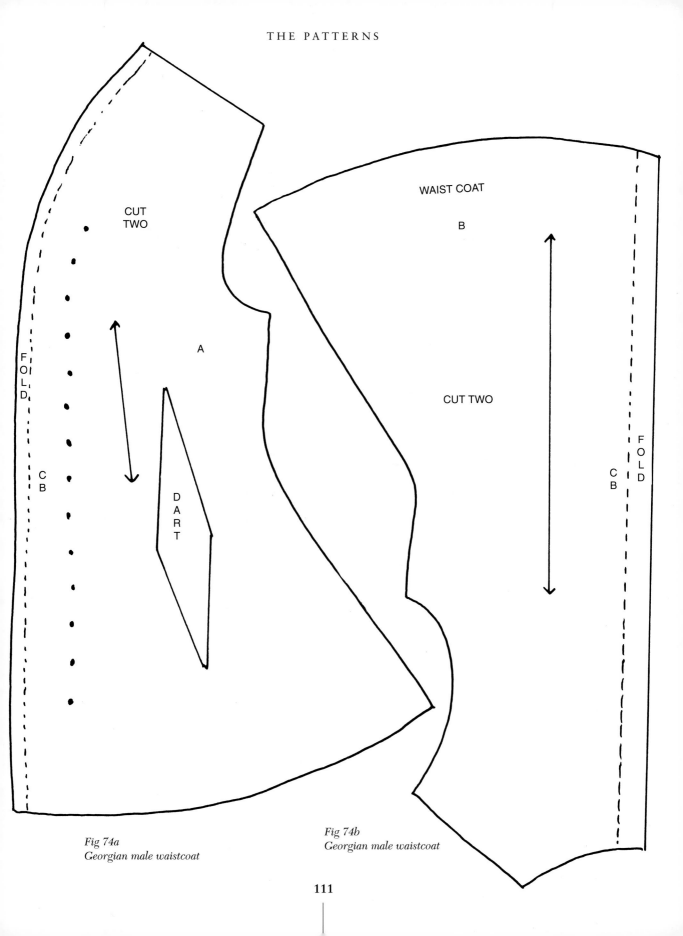

CUT
TWO

FOLD

CB

A

DART

WAIST COAT

B

CUT TWO

CB

FOLD

Fig 74a
Georgian male waistcoat

Fig 74b
Georgian male waistcoat

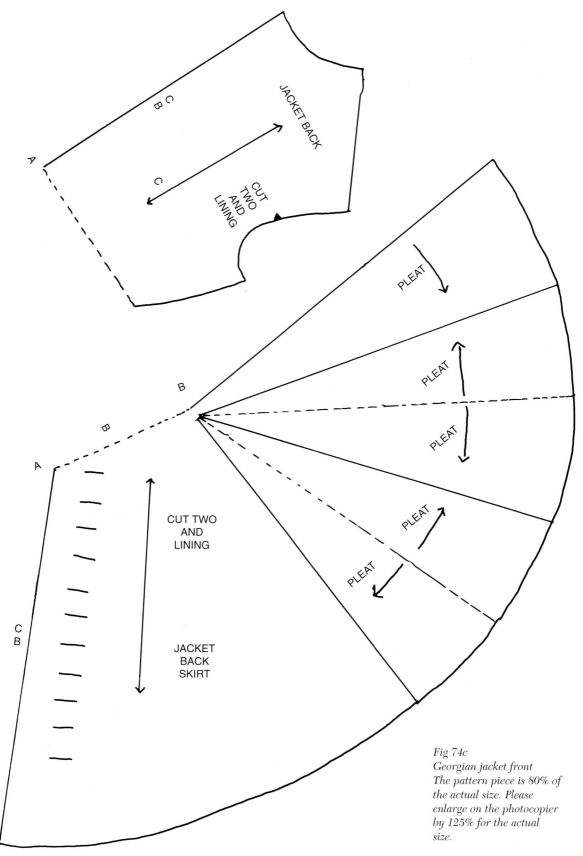

JACKET BACK

CUT TWO AND LINING

C
B C

C

A

B

A

B

PLEAT

PLEAT

PLEAT

PLEAT

PLEAT

PLEAT

CUT TWO
AND
LINING

JACKET
BACK
SKIRT

C
B

Fig 74c
Georgian jacket front
The pattern piece is 80% of
the actual size. Please
enlarge on the photocopier
by 125% for the actual
size.

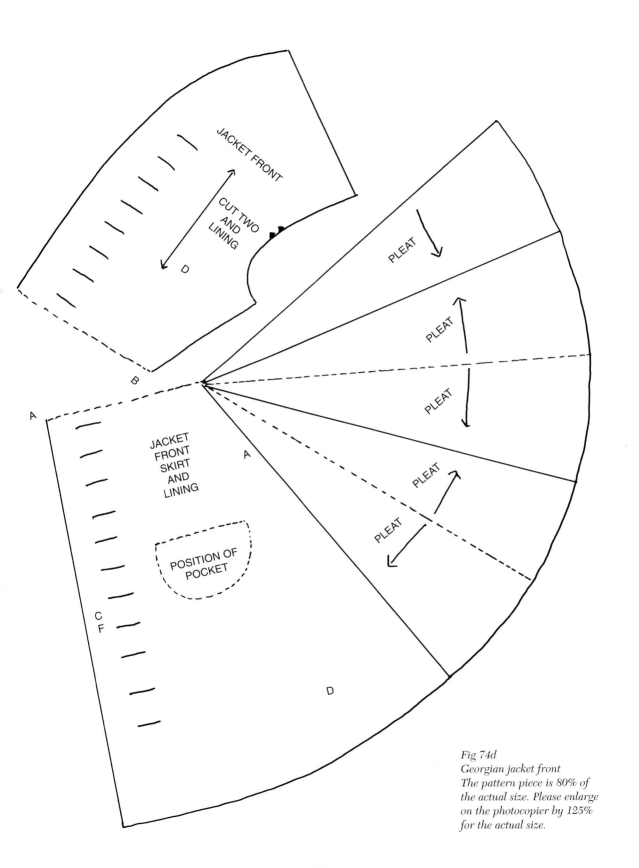

JACKET FRONT

CUT TWO
AND
LINING

D

B

A

JACKET
FRONT
SKIRT
AND
LINING

A

POSITION OF
POCKET

C
F

D

PLEAT

PLEAT

PLEAT

PLEAT

PLEAT

Fig 74d
Georgian jacket front
The pattern piece is 80% of
the actual size. Please enlarge
on the photocopier by 125%
for the actual size.

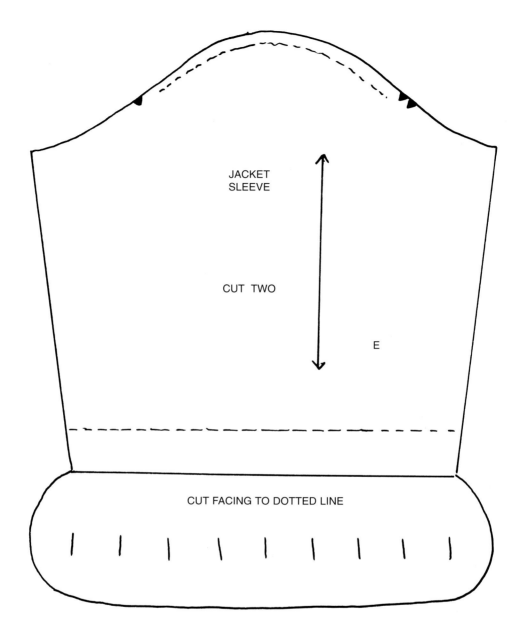

JACKET
SLEEVE

CUT TWO

E

CUT FACING TO DOTTED LINE

Fig 74e
Georgian jacket sleeve

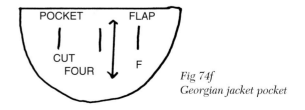

POCKET   FLAP

CUT

FOUR   F

Fig 74f
Georgian jacket pocket

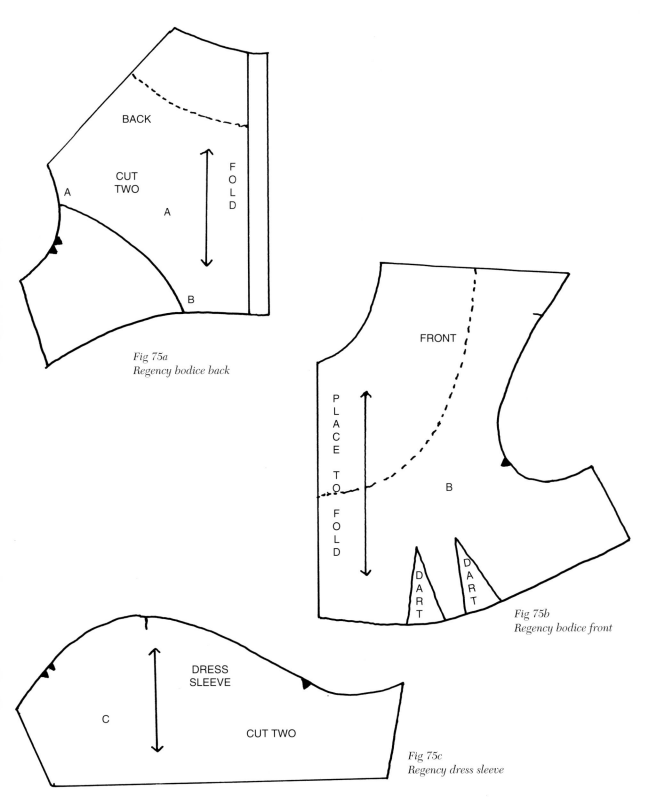

BACK

CUT
TWO

FOLD

A

A

B

Fig 75a
Regency bodice back

FRONT

PLACE TO FOLD

B

DART

DART

Fig 75b
Regency bodice front

DRESS
SLEEVE

C

CUT TWO

Fig 75c
Regency dress sleeve

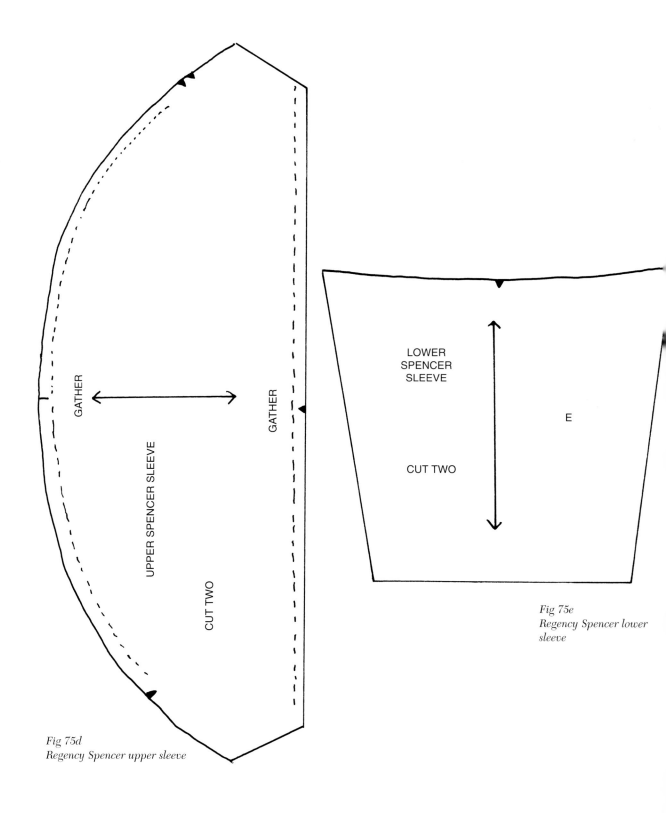

GATHER

GATHER

UPPER SPENCER SLEEVE

CUT TWO

LOWER
SPENCER
SLEEVE

E

CUT TWO

Fig 75d
Regency Spencer upper sleeve

Fig 75e
Regency Spencer lower sleeve

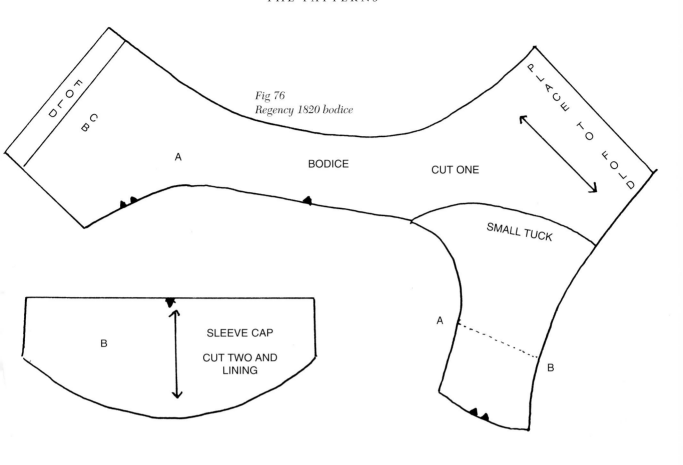

Fig 76
Regency 1820 bodice

FOLD

C

A

BODICE

CUT ONE

PLACE TO FOLD

SMALL TUCK

B

SLEEVE CAP

CUT TWO AND
LINING

A

B

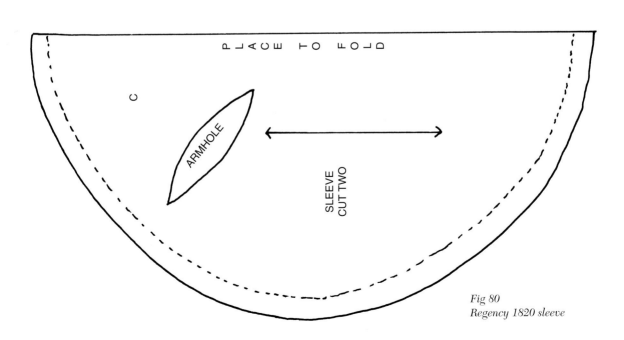

PLACE TO FOLD

C

ARMHOLE

SLEEVE
CUT TWO

Fig 80
Regency 1820 sleeve

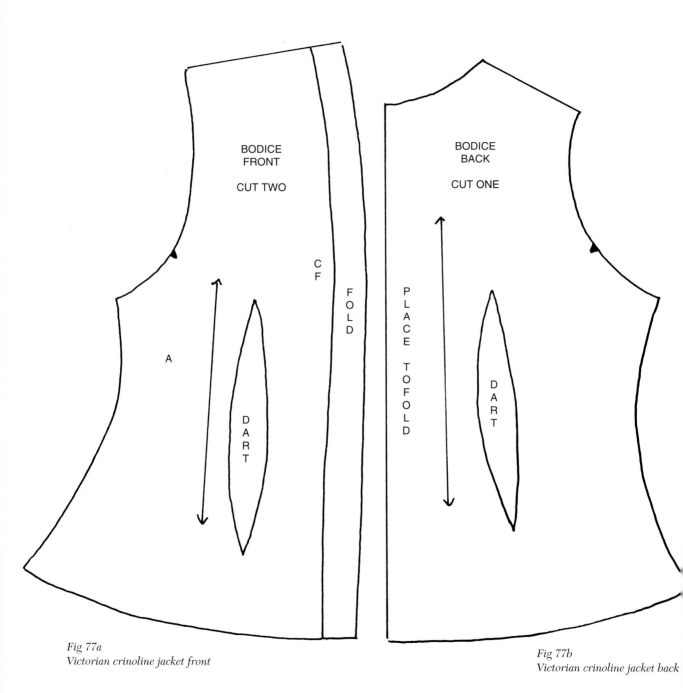

BODICE
FRONT

CUT TWO

BODICE
BACK

CUT ONE

C
F

F
O
L
D

P
L
A
C
E

T
O
F
O
L
D

A

D
A
R
T

D
A
R
T

Fig 77a
Victorian crinoline jacket front

Fig 77b
Victorian crinoline jacket back

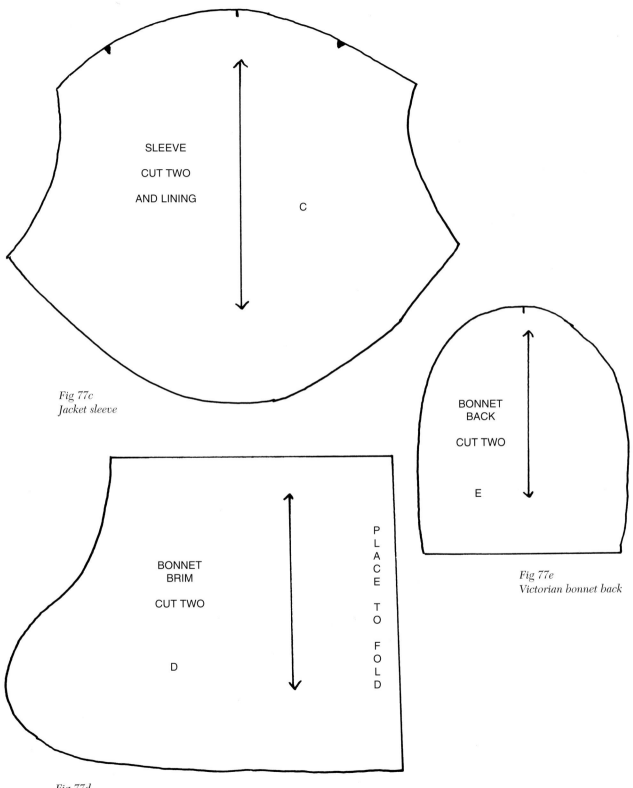

SLEEVE

CUT TWO

AND LINING

C

Fig 77c
Jacket sleeve

BONNET
BACK

CUT TWO

E

Fig 77e
Victorian bonnet back

BONNET
BRIM

CUT TWO

D

PLACE TO FOLD

Fig 77d
Victorian bonnet brim

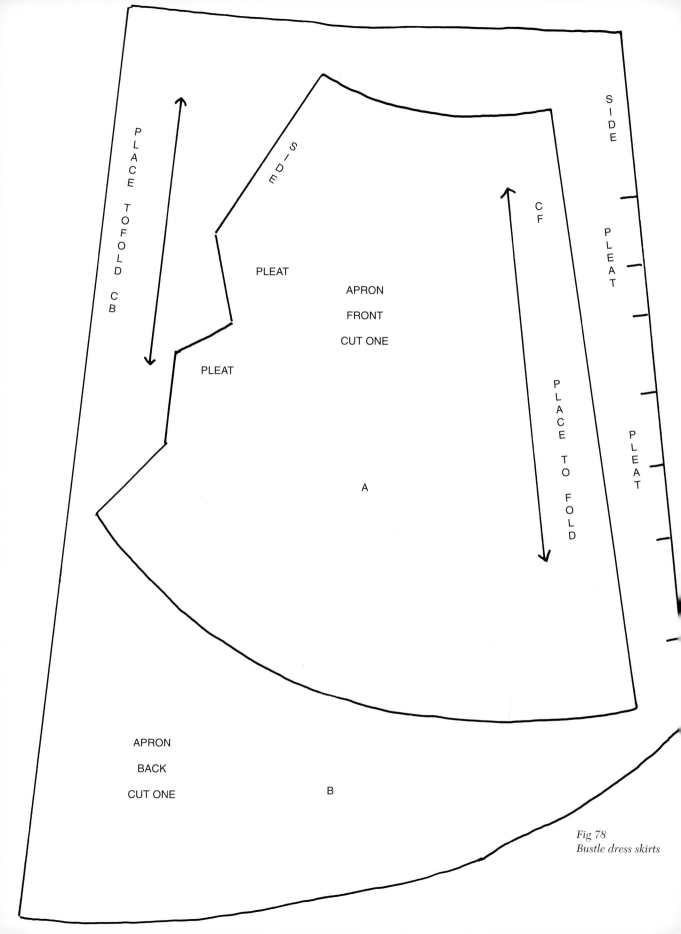

Fig 78
Bustle dress skirts

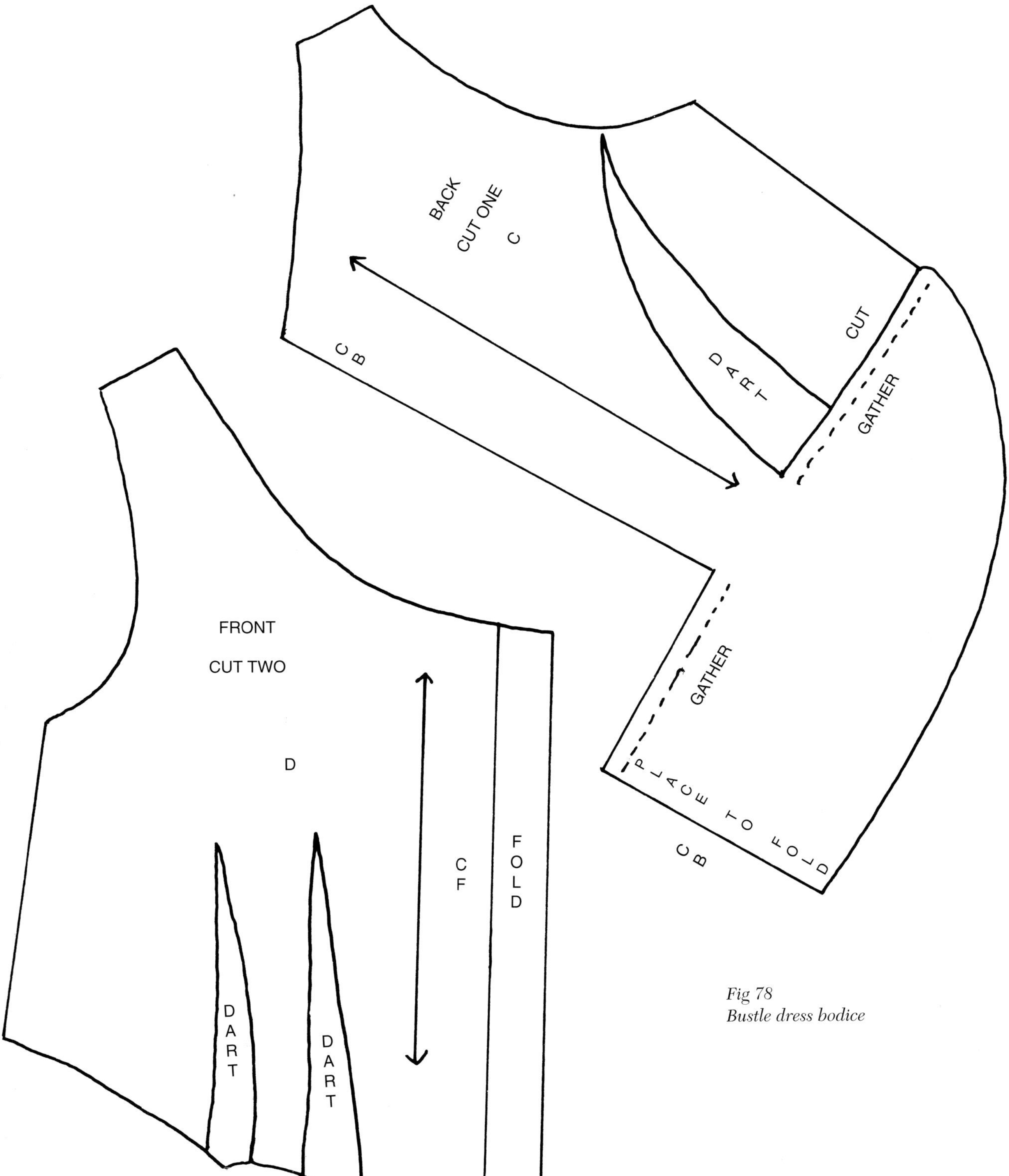

BACK

CUT ONE

C

C B

D A R T

CUT

GATHER

GATHER

P L A C E T O F O L D

C B

FRONT

CUT TWO

D

C F

F O L D

D A R T

D A R T

Fig 78
Bustle dress bodice

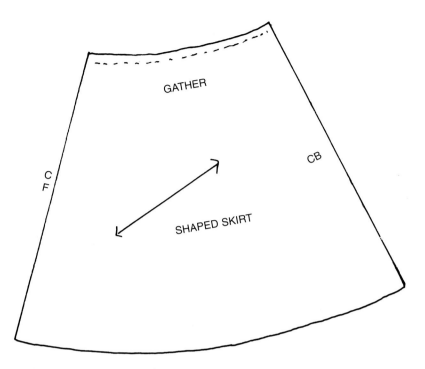

GATHER

CF

CB

SHAPED SKIRT

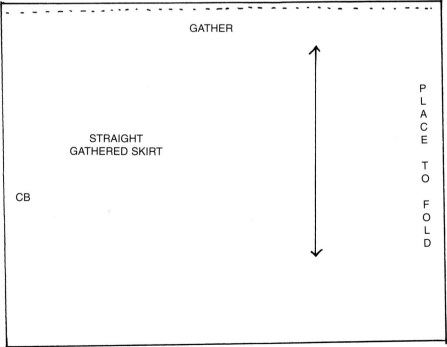

GATHER

STRAIGHT
GATHERED SKIRT

CB

PLACE TO FOLD

Fig 79
6 in doll skirts

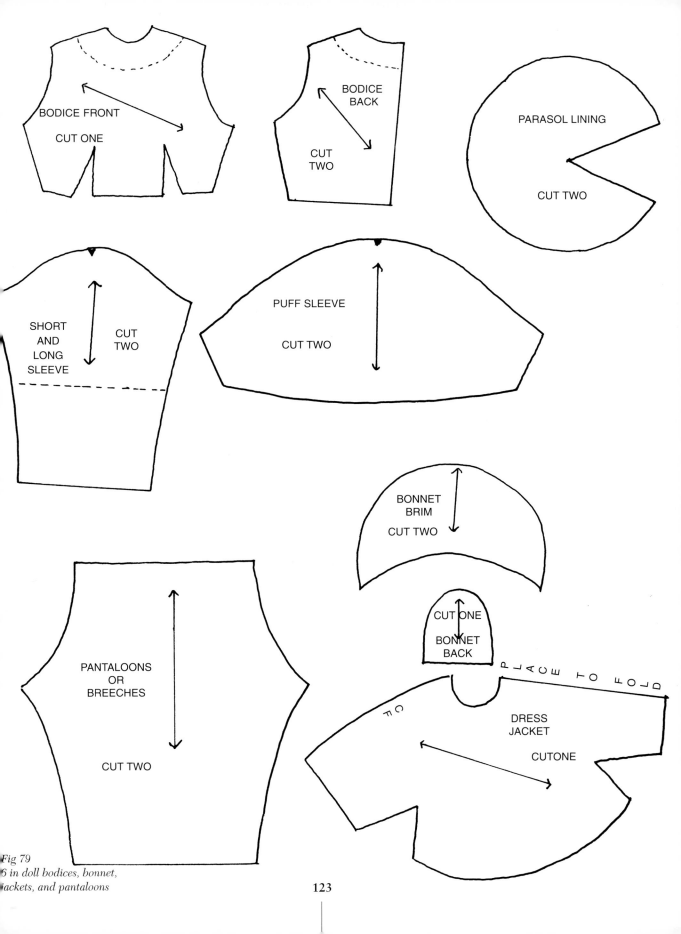

BODICE FRONT

CUT ONE

BODICE BACK

CUT TWO

PARASOL LINING

CUT TWO

SHORT AND LONG SLEEVE

CUT TWO

PUFF SLEEVE

CUT TWO

BONNET BRIM

CUT TWO

CUT ONE

BONNET BACK

PANTALOONS OR BREECHES

CUT TWO

PLACE TO FOLD

DRESS JACKET

CUTONE

CF

Fig 79
6 in doll bodices, bonnet,
jackets, and pantaloons

FURTHER READING

Atkinson, Sue, *Making and Dressing Doll's House Dolls in Twelve-Scale*, David and Charles (1992)

Arnold, Janet, *Patterns of Fashion, 1560 -1620*, Wace & Co. (1985)
Patterns of Fashion 1660 -1860, Wace & Co. (1964)
Patterns of Fashion 1860-1940, Wace & Co.

Collier, Ann, *Lace in Miniature*, Batsford (1994)

Courtais, Georgine de, *Women's Head-dress and Hair Styles*, Batsford (1973)

Earnshaw, Pat, *Lace in Fashion*, Batsford (1985)

Ewing, Elizabeth, *Everyday Dress, 1650-1900*, Batsford (1984)

Green, Vivien, *English Doll's Houses of the 18th and 19th century*, Bell and Hymen (1979)

Hill, Margot Hamilton and Bucknell, Peter A. *The Evolution of Fashion*, Batsford 1967

Morse, Michal, *Build a Doll's House*, Batsford (1993)
Furnish a Doll's House, Batsford (1994)

Wilcox, R Turner, *A Dictionary of Costume*, Batsford (1970)

SOURCES OF INFORMATION

UK

The Lace Guild
The Hollies
53 Audnam
Stourbridge
West Midlands DY8 4AE

The Lacemakers' Circle
49 Wardwick
Derby DE1 1HY

The Lace Society
Linwood
Stratford Raod
Oversley
Alcester
War BY9 6PG

The British College of Lace
21 Hillmorton Road
Rugby
War CV22 5DF

Ring of Tatters
Miss B Netherwood
269 Oregon Way
Chaddesden
Derby DE2 6UR

United Kingdom Director of
International Old Lacers
S Hurst
4 Dollis Road
London N3 1RG

USA

International Old Lacers
124 West Irvington Place
Denver
CO 80223-1539

Lace & Crafts magazine
3201 East Lakeshore Drive
Tallahassee
FL 32312-2034

OIDFA
(International Bobbin and
Needle Lace Organisation)
Kathy Kauffmann
1301 Greenwood
Wilmette
IL60091

LIST OF SUPPLIERS

England

BEDFORDSHIRE

A Sells
49 Pedley Lane
Clifton
Shefford SG17 5QT

BERKSHIRE

Chrisken Bobbins
26 Cedar Drive
Kingsclere RG20 5TD

BUCKINGHAMSHIRE

J S Sear
Lacecraft Supplies
8 Hillview
Sherington MK16 9NJ

Winslow Bobbins
70 Magpie Way
Winslow MK18 3PZ
SMP
4 Garners Close
Chalfont St Peter SL9 OHB

CAMBRIDGESHIRE

Josie and Jeff Harrison
Walnut Cottage
Winwick
Huntingdon PE17 5PN

Heffers Graphic Shop
(matt coloured transparent
adhesive film)
19 Sidney Street
Cambridge CB1 1LN

Spangles
(beads)
Carole Morrs
Casburn Lane
Burwell CB5 OED

CHESHIRE

Lynn Turner
Church Meadow Crafts
7 Woodford Lane
Winsford CW7 2JS

DERBYSHIRE

Georgina Dolls (16-20 in dolls)
173 Allestree Lane
Allestree
Derby DE3 2PG

The Dolls' House Emporium
(dolls' houses, furniture and
accessories)
Victoria Road
Ripley
Derbyshire DE5 3YD

DEVON

Honiton Lace Shop
44 High Street
Honiton EX14 8PJ

DORSET

Frank Herring & Sons
27 High West Street
Dorchester DT1 1UP

T Parker
(mail-order, general and
bobbins, small fan frames)
124 Corhampton Road
Boscombe East
Bournemouth BH6 5NZ

ESSEX

Needlework
Ann Bartleet
Bucklers Farm
Coggershall CO6 1SB

GLOUCESTERSHIRE

Chosen Crafts Centre
46 Winchcombe Street
Cheltenham GL52 2ND

HAMPSHIRE

Richard Viney (bobbins)
Unit 7
Port Royal Street
Southsea PO5 3UD

ISLE OF WIGHT

Busy Bobbins
Unit 7
Scarrots Lane
Newport PO30 1JD

KENT

The Handicraft Shop
47 Northgate
Canterbury CT1 1BE

Denis Hornsby
25 Manwood Avenue
Canterbury CT2 7AH

Francis Iles
73 High Street
Rochester ME1 1LX

Ann Lucas (small ½ scale doll
kits)
World of my Own
18 London Road
Farningham
Kent DA4 OJP

LANCASHIRE

Malcolm J Fielding (bobbins)
2 Northern Terrace
Moss Lane
Silverdale LA5 OST

LINCOLNSHIRE

Ken and Pat Schultz
Whynacres
Shepeau Stow
Whaplode Drove
Spalding PE12 OTU

LONDON

Sunday dolls
(1/12 scale dolls)
7 Park Drive
East Sheen SW14 8RB

MERSEYSIDE

Redburn Crafts
Squires Garden Centre
Halliford Road
Upper Halliford
Shepperton TW17 8RU

NORFOLK

Stitches and Lace
Alby Craft Centre
Cromer Road
Alby
Norwich NR11 7QE

Jane's Pincushions
Taverham Craft Unit 4
Taverham Nursery Centre
Fir Covert Road
Taverham
Norwich NR8 6HT

SOUTH YORKSHIRE

D H Shaw
47 Lamor Crescent
Thrushcroft
Rotherham S66 9QD

STAFFORDSHIRE

J & J Ford
(mail-order and lace days only)
October Hill
Upper Way
Upper Longdon
Rugeley WS15 1QB

SUFFOLK

A R Archer
The Poplars
Shetland
Nr Stowmarket IP14 3DE

Mary Collins
(linen by the metre, and made
up articles of church linen)
Church Furnishings
St Andrews hall
Humber Doucy Lane
Ipswich IP4 3BP

E & J Piper
(silk, embroidery and lace
thread)
Silverlea
Flax Lane
Glemsford CO10 7RS

SURREX

Southern Handicrafts
20 Kensington Gardens
Brighton BN1 4AC

WARWICKSHIRE

Christine & David Springett
21 Hillmorton Road
Rugby CV22 5DF

Weddington Woodfarm Crafts
(threads, evenweave linen and
fine lawn)
Woodfarm
Watling Street
Weddington
Nuneaton
Warwickshire CV10 OTX

WEST MIDLANDS

Framecraft
83 Hampstead Road
Handsworth Wood
Birmingham B2 1JA

The Needlewoman
21 Needles Alley
Off New Street
Birmingham B2 5AE

WEST YORKSHIRE

The Dolls' House Draper
(dolls' haberdashery)
PO Box 128
Lightcliffe
Halifax HX34 8RN

Jo Firth
Lace Marketing & Needlecraft
Supplies
58 Kent Crescent
Lowtown
Pudsey LS28 9EB

Just Lace
Lacemaker Supplies
14 Ashwood Gardens
Gildersome
Leeds LS27 7AS

Sebalace
Waterloo Mills
Howden Road
Silsden BD20 OHA

George White Lacemaking
Supplies
40 Heath Drive
Boston Spa LS23 6PB

WILTSHIRE

Doreen Campbell
(frames and mounts)
Highcliff
Bremilham Road
Malmesbury SN16 ODQ

Scotland

Christine Riley
The Embroiderer's Shop
53 Barclay Street
Stonehaven
Kincardineshire

Wales

Bryncraft Bobbins
B J Phillips
Pantglas
Cellan
Lampeter
Dyfed SA48 8JD

Hilkar Lace Suppliers
33 Mysydd Road
Landore
Swansea

Australia

Australian Lace magazine
PO Box 609
Manly
NSW 2095

Dentelles Lace Supplies
c/o Betty Franks
39 Lang Terrace
Northgate 4013
Brisbane
Queensland

The Lacemaker
724a Riversdale Road
Camberwell
Victoria 3124

Spindle and Loom
83 Longueville Road
Lane Cove
NSW 2066

Tulis Crafts
201 Avoca Street
Randwick
NSW 2031

New Zealand

Peter McLeavey
PO Box 69007
Auckland 8

USA

Arbor House
22 Arbor Lane
Roslyn Heights
NY 11577

Baltazor Inc
3262 Severn Avenue
Metairie
LA 7002

Beggars' Lace
PO Box 481223
Denver
Colo 80248

Berga Ullman Inc
PO Box 918
North Adams
MA 01247

Happy Hands
3007 SW Marshall
Pendleton
Oreg 97180

International Old Lacers Inc
124 West Irvington Place
Denver
Colo 80223-1539

The Lacemaker
23732-G Bothell Hwy
SE Bothell
WA 98021

Lace Place de Belgique
800 S W 17th Street
Boca Raton
FL 33432

Lacis
3163 Adeline Street
Berkeley
CA 94703

Robin's Bobbins
RTI Box 1736
Mineral Bluff
GA 30559-9736

Robin and Russ Handweavers
533 North Adams Street
McMinnville
Oreg 97128

The Unique and Art Lace
Cleaners
5926 Delman Boulevard
St Louis
MO 63112

Unicorn Books
Glimakra Looms 'n Yarns Inc
1304 Scott Street
Petalurna
CA 94954-1181

Van Sciver Bobbin Lace
130 Cascadilla Park
Ithaca
NY 14850

The World in Stitches
82 South Street
Milford
NH 03055

INDEX